If Life Is
ALL JOY
Why Am I Sad?

If Life Is
ALL JOY
Why Am I Sad?

by
Dianne E. Balch

Here's Life Publishers, Inc.
San Bernardino, California

**If Life Is
ALL JOY
Why Am I Sad?**

by Dianne E. Balch

Published by HERE'S LIFE PUBLISHERS, INC.
P. O. Box 1576
San Bernardino, CA 92402

Library of Congress Catalogue Card 82-72303
ISBN 0-86605-098-1
HLP Product No. 40-306-3
© Copyright 1982, Here's Life Publishers, Inc.

Printed in the United States of America

Unless otherwise indicated, Scripture quotations are from the New American Standard Bible, © The Lockman Foundation 1960, 1962, 1963, 1968, 1971, 1972, 1973, 1975, and are used by permission.

Cover Photo: Don Valentine

This book is dedicated to Nancy S. DeMoss and her beloved, departed husband, Arthur.

They impressed us with their love, challenged us with their vision, encouraged us in our growth, and blessed us with the opportunity to serve Jesus Christ with them on Philadelphia's Main Line.

We have counted it ALL JOY!

CONTENTS

Preface

IT TOOK a fiery trial in my life to cause me to wonder how I could "consider it all joy," the commandment given in the first chapter of the Book of James. The lessons were not learned overnight. I came through the trial with the conviction that the treasures locked in this concept have set me free to help others count it all joy—even when life is overwhelming and our struggles force us to question, *all* joy, Lord?

With a husband, two teenagers, an 87-year-old grandmother living with us, Katchoo the cat, and a multi-faceted ministry of outreach and discipling, it should be apparent that I'm not *looking* for a way to spend time! Daring to blaze this new trail of service for my Lord is simply an attempt not to limit what God might choose to do through my life.

This study in the Book of James was first presented as lectures to the women of the Creative Living Bible Study on Philadelphia's Main Line. Several hundred women make up this inter-denominational group, and they have said that studying James contributed significantly to their life-changing walk with Christ.

When I inquired to see if several women in the group would help transcribe the taped lectures, the responses encouraged me to persevere. Mary Knake, who assisted me in this, remarked that the study had meant so much to her. Her young daughter was recently called to Heaven after living for years with congenital heart disease. Mary is practicing "considering it all joy." Typing these transcripts has hopefully "called to remembrance" the paths to joy and peace, even with heartache and grief present.

Another friend, Bonnie Macaleer, joyfully accepted a tape to transcribe, reflecting on the horrible depression from which she had been lifted as she studied James and applied God's principles to her life.

When the book of James was written, the Jews were·experiencing intense persecution. Many were being killed. Our trials today take on many different forms, but they are just as real. As I taught from James, I learned three general truths about the Word of God:

First, every passage in the Bible is about relationships. We will spend a lifetime learning to relate effectively horizontally and vertically because it does not come naturally! It takes God's power to succeed.

Second, the Bible is an instruction manual which reveals principles of truth that transcend history and cultural barriers. Whether we are being thrown to the lions or are trying to sit through a meal with a tired mate and two normal teenagers, these concepts work!

How many of us have tried for years to put our lives together without checking with the manufacturer? Suddenly, after reading the instruction manual, we discover the reason for our malfunctions: we're missing a few nuts and bolts. As we place our lives in the manufacturer's hands, He doesn't merely replace and oil a few old parts. He makes us new from the inside out!

Third, the Bible says as much about trials and suffering as it does about joy and blessing. Some of us are slow to realize that life is a series of trials intertwined with God's love and forgiveness, and though we work sincerely on harmonious relationships while waiting for God's promises to be fulfilled, we don't want to admit that we need *all* of these to triumph in life's trials. We would rather wear rose-colored glasses!

Wearing them myself for more than thirty years, I simply refused to dwell upon the heartaches, pressures, and stresses that came my way. My rose-colored glasses were securely in place as I looked at the bright side of everything, sometimes through gritted teeth. Broken hearts, shattered homes, adultery, alcoholism, venereal disease, pregnancy out of wedlock, abortion, financial dilemma, drug addiction, psychiatric care, suicide (attempted and achieved), terminal illness, death, all touched me through relationships. But I swept them aside, refusing to see anything but the high points and the fun times. I was living "the good life."

It was hard for me to admit that I could not create a beautiful dream world by wearing those imaginary glasses.

But I finally learned. Before we moved to Philadelphia, God permitted a trial in my life that was devastating. It took time for wounds to heal and hope to stabilize. I didn't want to be a "spiritual casualty" though, and dogged determination to believe and apply God's Word consistently, regardless of feelings, got me through. It was there in the test tube of daily living, with an unalterable trial, that the secrets of considering it *all* joy became as tangible as a gold nugget.

As our ministry to the business and professional community in Philadelphia grew, we met hundreds of people at elegant evangelistic dinners held at country clubs and beautiful homes. Gradually, I watched sophisticated women draw closer to the gospel as they peeked out from *their* rose-colored glasses. I soon realized that behind the closed doors of these affluent homes were similar devastating, heartbreaking, self-esteem-shattering dramas being endured and lived out daily. As I talked with these women personally or at a Bible study, God equipped me to look into their weary eyes and find ways to say: "You, too, have carefully concealed the decay of a home that has no solid foundation. You, too, have let pride cause you to insist that the fantasy you've created is reality. You *can* take off your rose-colored glasses as I have and discover a dimension of life more real than all you see around you! It *is* possible to learn to consider it *all* joy!"

Recently, as I spoke at a women's coffee, I was explaining my "rose-colored glasses" attitude. Halfway through my talk, a woman leaned forward in her seat, tilted her head, removed her glasses and held them out for *all* to see. They were rose-colored! She had our attention. Quietly she explained that she had recently gone through a very painful divorce. During this time a friend of hers had teased that if she would switch to tinted glasses she might see a brighter world. She took that advice literally and invested in a pair. She liked the new outlook, but now she admitted she understood my point.

It is my desire that this study will challenge the reader to believe and love God's Word, to hunger and thirst after it, and to know the liberating power in obeying His instructions and experiencing His faithfulness.

Acknowledgments

THERE HAS been a new appreciation gained on my part for all of the author's acknowledgments I've read over the years. It always seems like a gracious gesture, but I failed to grasp the significance of what they were expressing until now.. So my enlightened and grateful acknowledgments are extended to:

My husband, who encouraged me not to wait for an idle time to pursue this project, since none exists.

To Mary Knake, who volunteered her services to transcribe a dozen casette tapes of my lectures, and then organized a team of women who stuck with the job and finished it. To Melodee Park, Bonnie Macaleer, Jeanne Hancock and Betty Shields, the members of that team, for their service and love.

Again, to Mary, who walked the extra mile. Besides typing my scribbled rewrites, she ministered to me personally. When quitting seemed both inviting and logical to me, Mary would phone to let me know that she or her husband, Roger, had been touched or challenged by something in my notes. She would admonish, "Keep writing, Dianne—you DO have something to say!"

To my grandmother, "NaNa," who, when she saw how burdensome and time-consuming the handwriting had become, gave me a nice portable electric typewriter.

To the Stulls, the MacLeans and the Camerons, who loaned our family their resort area homes so we could "come apart before we came apart." There, in secluded settings, much of this book was written. And there I became vividly aware of the support of Dave, Katie and David, who listened attentively when I needed a "sounding board," and just watched contentedly when I didn't.

To my secretary, Peggy Adams, who started working two days after we received word that the book had been accepted for publication. As the Lord provided her to help with the last six chapters, I could look back on His trail of provisions with childlike awe.

And finally, to Leslie H. Stobbe, Editorial Director of Here's Life Publishers, who walked this manuscript through the selection process and encouraged its acceptance (on their part) and completion (on my part).

What are authors saying when they acknowledge those who have helped bring a book to completion? From the Christian perspective, I think it is that we have caught a glimpse of the beautiful way the Body of Christ is designed by the Master Designer to work. We encourage each other (and innumerable friends have encouraged me) as we believe in each other, and we blend our skills to see Christ exalted. I am deeply grateful to be a part of a team of God's children who labor to serve and glorify Him — and Him alone.

James, a bond-servant of God and of the Lord Jesus Christ, to the twelve tribes who are dispersed abroad, greetings.

Consider it all joy, my brethren (James 1:1,2).

PART I

Choosing God's Path of Joy

Chapter 1

All Joy, Lord?
James 1:1,2

1 James, a bond-servant of God and of the Lord Jesus Christ, to the twelve tribes who are dispersed abroad, greetings.

2 Consider it all joy, my brethren, when you encounter various trials,

"LAST CALL for Bismarck!" a voice crackled over the intercom.

Paying little attention to the airport noises, I intently studied the papers in my lap. They were outlines on four messages I was going to deliver in Bismarck on the book of James. I intended to explain that James instructs us *how* to be joyful, in difficult situations, where it seems impossible to imagine anything resembling joy.

Suddenly, I realized what I had just heard. "Last call for Bismarck?" How could that be! I'm *in* Bismarck. I jumped out of the waiting room seat, my heart pounding rapidly. I frantically stuffed the outlines into my attaché case, threw on my winter coat, and grabbed the three heavy pieces of luggage.

Glancing around, I could see only an armed security guard standing behind a glass partition. I struggled over to the glass wall, dropped one piece of luggage, and knocked emphatically to get his attention. When he looked my way, I yelled, "Where am I?"

Prayers were streaming vertically as he opened his door to help with my problem.

"Where am I," I asked again.

He'll think I'm crazy, I thought. *We're supposed to know where we are!*

"Fargo? I'm in *Fargo?* But, I thought we landed in *Bismarck!*"

Smiling sadly, the guard shook his head. I was dumbfounded. Then my questions exploded like a string of firecrackers. "Where's the plane I was on? What? On its way to Bismarck? When does the *next* plane leave? *This* is the final plane to Bismarck? Where can I buy a ticket? Will you hold the plane?"

Lord, can this really be happening? How could I have missed staying on the plane to Bismarck?

I dashed to the other end of the Fargo terminal, hauling my suitcase, book bag, and attaché. Little did I realize that this trip to speak at a women's retreat in Bismarck, North Dakota, would turn out to be a test of that principle set forth in James. I had pulled together eight months' notes and transparencies to tell others how to live joyfully in the midst of their trials. And now, I was being challenged to live by my own teachings.

Arriving at the ticket counter, I had perspiration dripping off my nose, but a smile on my face as I explained my dilemma. Thanks to Master Charge and the grace of God, I once again ran the full length of the terminal with all my gear and a ticket between my teeth . . .

This effort had been a challenge from the start. At home in Philadelphia the airline had overbooked and, although I had a ticket, I was placed on stand-by. Hobbling toward the boarding gate, I had struggled with a two-hundred-pound suitcase containing half my wardrobe, a fifty-pound book bag full of commentaries, a Bible and several unfinished books, and the messages in my attaché which weighed a ton.

But by the time I reached the gate, I had cast "all [my] anxiety on the Lord" (1 Peter 5:7). It was interesting during the next half-hour to watch the struggles going on in others, sometimes erupting into confrontations with the airline employees. It was also fascinating to see how, at the very last minute, the Lord placed me on that plane when many others were left behind.

Because of snow we had arrived in Chicago late. I seized all the gear and rushed from one terminal to the next, barely making my connection. I sank gratefully into my seat on the plane, and soon realized I was sitting next to a "divine appointment." The young man was an elder in his church but did not know Christ personally. During the flight, we talked seriously about Jesus. As the plane descended and the stewardess announced something about Bismarck, I was urging him to open his heart and receive the Lord.

Disembarking from the plane, I strolled casually into the airport waiting room, hunting for Chris, the friend who was to meet me. She was nowhere in sight. I called her home and received no answer. *She must be on her way,* I thought. *She must have many details to tie down before leaving her husband and two boys for the weekend. Bless her heart!*

Since my first lecture was to be delivered in less than two hours, it had looked like a perfect time to go over my notes. It didn't take long to shed my warm coat, drop down into a seat in the waiting area, open the attaché, and spread out my outlines. This was fun! As businessmen occasionally glanced over, I mused that they would never guess that I was on a mission for the God of the universe. Bet none of *them* served a King!

"Last call for Bismarck."

There! The finishing touches on the first message were complete. My text was James 1:2,3 — "Consider it all joy, my brethren, when you encounter various trials, knowing that the testing of your faith produces endurance," or, as the King James version puts it, "Count it all joy...knowing this, that the trying of your faith worketh patience." It might be possible to condense two months' of lectures into that first hour, if I stuck to the outline . . .

What's he talking about — "Last call for Bismarck?" We're in Bismarck!

That's when I learned from the security guard that I was really in Fargo. No wonder Chris hadn't answered my call. I was calling her in the wrong city!

As I raced toward the boarding gate, I wondered, *How am I going to teach "count it all joy" if I can't pass the test myself?* The choice was clear. I could cry, "Lord, why is this happening to me?" or I could count it *all* joy and believe that God would work the situation for good. The Lord didn't want a phony delivering those messages.

The security guard shared my relief as I galloped toward the waiting plane, and I was about to learn why the Lord would put me through all of this to get to Bismarck.

Out of breath, I lunged into the plane, and headed toward the one vacant seat between two other passengers. As I collapsed into it, I realized that the lady on the aisle was my friend Gyneth, the vocalist from Indiana. She was asleep, so I leaned over and kissed her cheek. As her eyes popped open and she realized who I was, she started talking a mile a minute, in ecstatic joy! "Dianne! I can't believe it! Sit down! Meet Bob! I've been telling him *all* about our retreat and *all* about you and Dave and how you found the Lord. But I'm out of the Four Laws booklets, and I've taken him as far as I can. Will you talk to him?"

Turning to this young man, I soon saw that he truly was eager to know Christ personally. The groundwork had been done, so during our short 20 minute flight from Fargo to Bismarck, I read him the Four Spiritual Laws and he prayed to receive Christ. As we were landing, I gave him a booklet called *How to Be Sure You're a Christian* to help start his walk with Christ. As we shook hands and departed, I realized that a powerful, sovereign God had engineered a most unusual trip because of His redeeming love for a man named Bob.

Arriving at the retreat on time I marveled again at how incredible it is that God works through us and uses us to accomplish His purposes! I was thrilled that my decision to consider it *all* joy throughout the day had made me "usable" on that last leg of the trip! We all love a good "war story," and I'll *always* treasure this one — God's victory at Fargo!

Often we have a preconceived, erroneous concept of what joy really is. "Consider it all joy, my brethren, when you encounter various trials..." James wrote that joy is a fruit of the Spirit — a manifestation of the essence of God's character. God is love. He is the Prince of Peace. And God is Joy. (see Galatians 5:22). In urging us to trust and obey Him, Jesus added: "These things I have spoken to you, that My joy may be in you, and that your joy may be made full" (John 15:11).

It was when I was learning to consider it all joy that I first understood what joy is *not*. Joy is *not* a feeling. It is not a hilarious emotion that grips us when we join foot-stomping Christians in a chorus of "I've got the joy-joy-joy-joy down in my heart." Jesus "for the *joy* set before Him, endured the cross, despising the shame" (Hebrews 12:2). He knew the deep, abiding joy of the Spirit as He walked in obedience through His trials and suffering. But there was no happy emotion as He faced the cross!

As I have been rewriting my original lectures, the Lord has brought home to me emphatically that joy is not a feeling. It is an <u>act of the will, in spite of emotions.</u>

Joy is

<u>Joy is based upon forgiveness and vital, obedient fellowship with God.</u> Joy is independent of our circumstances and is meant to flourish and to be nourished in times of affliction. <u>It is the outcome of believing God's promises, *knowing* that His character is at stake</u>—and seeing that He always proves true. "Do not be grieved, for the joy of the Lord is your strength" (Nehemiah 8:10). If the joy of the Lord truly *is* the source of our strength—especially in trials—should we not heed His command and *not* be grieved, but instead consider it all joy? When we do, we experience, not necessarily a feeling, but an undefinable, deep awareness of the presence of God powerfully at work in us. It may be quiet, and it may be inexpressible, but it is real.

James (in the King James version) explains that trials are not something we've counted on and planned to have happen. They're compared to a fall. Have you ever planned a fall? Unless you're sadistic, you don't. If you fall, it's by accident and unexpected. If you see a confrontation about to take place, you brace yourself for the impact. If you have time, you prepare yourself mentally, physically and emotionally to respond properly. But in falling we're talking about the kinds of trials that hit, usually in multiples, when we least expect them. We're caught off balance.

Let's begin our quest for practical, joyful Christian living by studying James line by line and verse by verse. Let's pick at words and poke at phrases until they take on some practical meaning. It's been said that "repetition aids learning," so I won't apologize for repeating a verse or passage in our study. As we do this, God's Word will sink deeply into our hearts! Whether we're beginners or long time students of the Bible, we all need a reservoir of God's truth to draw upon daily in our pressure-packed world.

> James, a bond-servant of God and of the Lord Jesus Christ, to the twelve tribes who are dispersed abroad, greetings (James 1:1).

James was committed to serve God, not man. He prized his identity with God above all. Do we prize our identity with God above all, or do we place more merit on our family name, academic achievement, occupational title or address?

". . . To the *twelve tribes*---" There was a remnant of true believers represented in each of the twelve tribes of Israel.

". . . Which are dispersed abroad, *greetings*." Having touched on the fact that intense persecution was the reason for the scattering, it is amazing to discover that the more accurate translation for the word "greetings" would be "rejoice." In this opening sentence James points immediately to the Christian paradox of having a rejoicing heart in the midst of facing the reality of trials—in their case, severe persecution!

> Consider it all joy, my brethren, when you encounter various trials. . . . (James 1:2)

James is addressing believers in Jesus Christ, not the world at large. He speaks of a family relationship when he calls them "brethren." It was established when they personally appropriated John 1:12: "But as many as *received* Him [Jesus Christ], to them He gave the right [the authority] to *become* children of God, *even* to those who believe in [trust in, rely upon and adhere to] His name." They *became* something they weren't before, by the act of *receiving* Christ. Many of them had been very religious Jews. They had been "playing temple" the way I "played church" for so long! But they had not *become* something they weren't before: children of God. As children of God, what did that make them to each other? Brothers. What a special relationship! Special, because it hinged on the supernatural and what their mutual heavenly Father had done *in* their lives. "Christ in you, the hope of Glory" (Colossians 1:27).

When we read through these verses and look to other Scriptures, we soon see that to live above life's circumstances depends on God's *indwelling* presence and power. Unless we are truly one of the "brethren" we'll end up imitating. We'll read and then try to apply some principle of truth like the power of positive thinking. And you know something? It will work—to a point. But without the *indwelling* power of God, we will grow weary. We must draw upon the supernatural, indwelling, enabling power of God to see the consistent reality of His principles. And to do that, we must first be God's children.

The supernatural, enabling power of God—this is what we all want to tap into, isn't it? Not just cranking out an imitation of Christian life, but tapping into the resurrection power of the Christ who dwells within us by faith. Ten years ago the contents of a presentation of the gospel revealed to me that I was not a Christian, though I had exhausted myself while assuming that

I was! It showed me *how* I could become one. Knowing you are God's child — not an imitator — is a prerequisite to counting it all joy succesfully, and enjoying the benefits of applying the teachings in James.

"Consider it joy, my brethren, when you encounter various trials. . . ." That's what your Bible says, right? Wrong! It says, "Consider it(all)joy, my brethren when you encounter various trials. . . ." Big difference! We can circle the word *all*. All is a mouthful, and a part of us doesn't want that word to be there. What we really want God to say is, "Honey, consider it joy until the going gets rough and then I don't mind if you complain and grumble a bit." We want God to say, "Count it joy when you feel like it and when the bottom starts to fall out and you see the sides caving in, I expect you to go to pieces. Who wouldn't?" But that is not what He says.

God may at first seem audacious as He repeatedly makes *absolute* statements declaring *absolute* truth. In today's world, humanistic thinkers tell us there are no "absolutes." That makes it easy to rationalize. But the Word says there are "absolutes" and this particular statement says, "consider it *all* joy" with *no* excuses!

God did not permit James to get carried away or to exaggerate for the sake of emphasis in this second verse of his letter. The Lord knew how to make His point — repeatedly — through those who wrote over a period of 2,500 years! How clearly and boldly God challenges us to His *absolute,* holy standard with no "buts" about it!

To get a handle on how adamant God is in making all-inclusive, no-two-ways-about-it statements that He wants us to accept as *absolute* truth, you might pick up a pencil and do a bit of marking. Read the following verses and circle the words or phrases that are "absolutes."

"I, even I, am the Lord; and there is no savior besides Me" (Isaiah 43:11).

All of us like sheep have gone astray, each of us has turned to his own way; but the Lord has caused the iniquity of us all to fall on Him (Isaiah 53:6).

"Come to Me, all who are weary and heavy-laden, and I will give you rest" (Matthew 11:28).

And He said to him, "You shall love the Lord your God with all your heart, and with all your soul, and with all your mind" (Matthew 22:37).

And He said to them, "Go into all the world and preach the gospel to all creation" (Mark 16:15).

"All that the Father gives Me shall come to Me, and the one who comes to Me I will certainly not cast out" (John 6:37).

And my God shall supply all your needs according to His riches in glory in Christ Jesus (Philippians 4:19).

So that you may walk in a manner worthy of the Lord, to please Him in all respects, bearing fruit in every good work and increasing in the knowledge of God (Colossians 1:10).

Abstain from every form of evil (1 Thessalonians 5:22).

All Scripture is inspired by God and profitable for teaching, for reproof, for correction, for training in righteousness; that the man of God may be adequate, equipped for every good work (2 Timothy 3:16, 17).

In only ten verses I circled twenty-nine words or phrases, knowing with each stroke of my pencil that these are life-changing declarations of God's will and provision for me! It's revealing and convicting, isn't it, to grasp, through these few verses, that God consistently declares "absolutes" with boldness? The Scripture is full of them! And in this study we will accumulate many more.

God means business with us! Someone who speaks so clearly doesn't need an interpreter. So, getting back to our verse, when the good Lord said, "Consider it all joy, my brethren when you encounter various trials," that's exactly what He means. And we must choose to *do* it as an act of the will, if we wish to obey God and discover the victory of His ways.

Through these experiences called "various trials" the Lord encourages us to learn, understand and apply some principles in His Word repeatedly, so our heart reaction and our verbal response *can* be to consider it all joy consistently! It's *totally* impossible unless we're willing to practice choosing to obey, and the one who commands it supernaturally enables us to obey. And I've discovered, sometimes through tears, that He *will* when I *do!*

Now, just what is it that we are supposed to *do* to "consider it *all joy*"? The instruction is clear that we are to practice through "various trials" . . . I call them "the charge of the mosquitoes." But *how* is this accomplished?

Here are specific responses to trials which I have found effective in considering it all joy. In the areas of:

Thanksgiving

1 Thessalonians 5:16-19:

> Rejoice always.
> Pray without ceasing.
> In everything give thanks; for this is God's will for you
> in Christ Jesus.
> Do not quench the Spirit.

Claiming His promises

Romans 8:28:

> And we know that God causes all things to work together
> for good to those who love God, to those who are called
> according to His purpose.

Praise

Hebrews 13:15:

> Let us continually offer up a sacrifice of praise to God,
> that is, the fruit of lips that give thanks to His name.

These are practical ways to "consider it all joy." When we are new Christians, we can begin to consciously, daily *practice* until we see these responses to "various trials" becoming consistent, spontaneous reactions.

If we have known Christ personally for years, we probably *know* these promises well. We can quote these verses from memory eloquently because they are basic truths to the Christian walk. But are we practicing them? I don't mean mechanically with gritted teeth, for that is merely living in "hang-in-there," powerless defeat.

Occasionally God will permit "the charge of the mosquitoes" to expose our true reactions to trouble. It is truly humbling to realize that our spontaneous responses are not joy, prayer, giving thanks, trusting, leaning not on our own understanding or praise. He will let us hear ourselves grumble, whine, grit our teeth and complain. Then He will lovingly, but firmly, remind us to practice counting it all joy. The power won't be imparted until we practice. And this can come only with the daily pressures of life.

I remember one time when my practicing failed miserably.

My grandmother NaNa had been in the hospital for ten days. We had prayed for her, given thanks, claimed God's promises, and felt full of joy and praise. Then came the mosquitoes.

Basketball and cheerleading practice, daily visits to the hospital, shopping errands, teaching, studying, phoning, counseling, meetings and church activities filled my week until Friday. We had planned a ski weekend for months and, as an answer to prayer, NaNa was released from the hospital. After getting her home and settled, I packed for the weekend. I shopped for groceries, took NaNa's lunch tray to her, and started the laundry before I picked up Ian and Jen at their school. They would be spending the next ten days with us while their parents were away.

The first charge arrived when the dryer broke. *Praise You, Lord,* I thought. *I'll just put the wet laundry into pillow cases and take it in the car and dry it at the mountaintop condominium.*

Second charge! The water heater sprang a big, spraying leak! The basement floor was flooding, and it was time to get Ian and Jen.

As I drove away, unable to reach my husband or either of the plumbers listed in his phone book, I prayed — "Lord, keep NaNa safe!" I sang to escape the creeping anxiety. By the time I returned with the children, the basement floor was covered with four inches of water. "Praise the Lord," we all chimed as we waded around the water heater trying to find the handle that turned off the flow. I wanted to be a good example to the children, but this was getting serious! My prayers were sounding more and more like SOS signals than faith!

Finally, I reached the wife of one of the plumbers. She promised that he would come as soon as possible. Our children, Katie and David, arrived home from school, and we packed the car while we waited. For twenty-five dollars the plumber turned the water off and advised that we would need a new heater, which would cost several hundred dollars.

Later, when my husband Dave came in, I quickly recapped the events of the nine pressure-packed hours of the day. So far, I *had* counted it all joy.

Then my sweetheart quietly responded, "Honey, you called the wrong plumber."

I blew my cork! Give thanks? No way! Claim it to work for good? I already had, and look what I got! A calm, cool, "You called the wrong plumber." What am I, a mind reader? I was doing the best I could! And where was *he* when I needed him?

Trust? Praise? Sure, sure. When I get cooled down, Lord. When I'm good and ready. But for now, forget it!

There! I had made my choice. God's love, joy, and peace flew out the window, obviously preceded by my patience. I was determined to be good and angry— and fume and sulk!

Dave reached the right plumber who told him how to plug the water heater himself. I flopped into the car surrounded by four children, NaNa, the cat, the wet laundry, the luggage, the food, and the dear man who had said, "You called the wrong plumber."

One too many mosquitoes had charged. I set my jaw for a perfectly miserable three-hour drive. All I could think of was wet laundry to dry, meals to prepare, dishes to wash, and a condominium to clean after seven of us tracked snow in all weekend. Was this someone's idea of fun? Then there was the wet basement awaiting our return.

It's <u>amazing</u> how difficult it can be to repent and "let go" <u>once we have cheered the flesh on to a victory over the Holy Spirit.</u> You see, "<u>the lust of the flesh" is simply desiring our own way</u> — <u>and once we've decided willfully to take over the throne of our lives, and reign, we often face struggle and defeat when we could have graciously stepped down and let King Jesus take His rightful place and give us the victory.</u> "The battle *is* the Lord's."

<u>When was I defeated?</u> When I focused on *all* the circumstances, thereby letting the battle become *mine!* " . . . Let us also lay aside every encumbrance, and the sin which so easily entangles us, and let us run *with* endurance [patience] the race that is set before us, fixing our eyes on Jesus . . ." (Hebrews 12:1, 2). We run with patience when we're counting it all joy, focusing on the Lord. Unencumbered and cleansed, we're running "a fixed race," for Jesus is author and finisher of our faith. I was defeated when I hauled around the weights (circumstances), harbored the sin (my reaction to the circumstances), took my eyes off of Jesus and quit practicing "the basics."

When did the victory come? When I was disgusted with the ugly person my precious family and two young friends had been compelled to travel with. Then I got on my knees and confessed my sins of rebellion, laid aside the weights and focused once again on Jesus—to thank Him—to praise Him—to trust Him.

This could have happened one minute after the choice to willfully sin. How sad when precious hours, even days or years are wasted by our rebellious spirits. The choice is ours. I pray often that my family and I daily will be given hearts that quickly repent. Life is too precious to spend needless time with our heels dug in — determined to be miserable, refusing to count it all joy.

Recently, God has given me a new opportunity to *practice!* Perhaps some of you are facing stressful situations with aging relatives and will empathize with my most recent opportunity to count it *all* joy.

My 86 year-old grandmother NaNa has been sick again. She has "fallen" into two unexpected illnesses, and one of these required hospitalization for 10 days. We all survived the rigors of the hospital visits. But this time her illness requires care at home.

Because of this added responsibility, I've been "falling," too. Why? It certainly has nothing to do with her as a person. We love her. She has not complained, fretted or bickered since she came to our home three years ago. In fact, she's called her third-floor apartment "a corner of heaven" and has always shown appreciation for any kindness we might do her. She has graced our home, and especially our children, with the presence of a white-haired, caring "NaNa" (*great*-grandmother to the kids). In today's transient, nursing-home society, many people miss the enjoyment of this precious relationship.

Why then is NaNa's failing health a "testing of my faith"? Quite honestly, I've always had an aversion to caring for elderly people. NaNa did it for years as a living. I grew up with memories of smelling age and death in her home. Also, I am not a nurse! Several women from the Bible study are, and I admire the true mercy and compassion they've demonstrated as they've come to help. I'm sure Dottie, Doris, Ginger, and Ellie are gifts from God "for such a time as this"! I've dreaded having to bathe and dress her when she can't do it for herself. My stomach is weak when it comes to clipping toenails she can no longer reach or applying the soaks several times a day to the raw, inflamed shingles that have broken out on her tired, old body. And, there is a looming fear that I may become house-bound — something my energetic, meeting-packed, people-oriented life would naturally avoid.

Since her arrival I have often prayed, declaring my willingness to care for her. I tried to deal in advance with my "preferences" of being free. Next door to my Christian neighbor Dottie is a 93 year-old man who takes walks daily, visibly reminding me that NaNa could be with us quite a while longer!

"The testing of my faith" is taking place at a gut level. Can I trust the grace of God to alter my schedule indefinitely, considering it all joy? Can I avoid the pity parties, the resentment of smells, medicines being administered, trays being delivered from the kitchen to the third floor, and the obligation to visit a bit when there's so much else to do?

The answer to my questions must be "yes"! God assures me that His grace *is* sufficient and He *will* provide the way to escape my temptations (2 Corinthians 12:9 and 1 Corinthians 10:13). But this is a *choice* I must make with my will repeatedly throughout every day. And when my emotions buckle and tears flow and my feelings try to get away with a temper tantrum, I must choose to submit them to the power of Christ, trusting the fruit of His Spirit to reign and overrule. I have to remember, joy is not a feeling.

"For the flesh sets its desire against the Spirit, and the Spirit against the flesh; for these are in opposition to one another, so that you may not do the things that you please." Galatians 5:17 would be pretty glum news were it not for the verse that precedes it! "But I say, walk by the Spirit, and you will not carry out the desire of the flesh." Notice the absolute? I have a choice. Sometimes I buckle and fail; but the choice remains, and with it the promise of grace and victory.

The final chapter on NaNa's life, or on my part in blessing it, is not yet written. God is ministering to me through His people. Oswald Chambers once wrote in a devotional, "If in the externals of your life you live up to the highest you know, God will continually say: 'Friend, go up higher.' Growth in grace is measured not by the fact that you have gone back, but that you have an *insight into where you are* spiritually." That encourages me. I want to live up to all my Lord has shown me. I'm confessing the insight to my weakness when I fall back in squeamish resistance. By eagerly claiming His cleansing (1 John 1:9), choosing to obey and giving thanks in all things (1 Thessalonians 5:18), I am learning to thank Him for the painful disclosure of self! We don't like admitting our weaknesses, do we?

Trials and testings are a part of life. We are going to run into storms. Because of the nature of this world, rain and wind are unavoidable. But Jesus has given us a choice as to how to react.

The Lord won't let us *talk* these principles if we're not willing to *walk* them. He wants us to live our messages about His truths consistently. We cannot rationalize, "that's the way I am," if it's not the way Jesus is! God has promised to work it *all* together for good as He conforms us to the image of His Son (Romans 8:28, 29). He has provided ways for us to consider it all joy, even when we tumble unexpectedly into stressful situations.

Reflect and Act

Perhaps there is an area of your life which you need to surrender to the Lord. You may want to use the following as a definite step of commitment:

Lord Jesus, I *choose* to count it *all* joy. Forgive me and cleanse me from the sin of_____. I trust You with my situation. Thank You for _____. I trust You to harness my feelings, knowing they will eventually catch up with my choice to count it all joy. I claim Your promise to_____. I praise You from the bottom of my heart for where You have me right now. Amen.

Signed _____

Chapter 2

Trials: God's Appointed Way Forward
James 1:2, 3

2 Consider it all joy, my brethren, when you encounter various trials, 3 knowing that the testing of your faith produces endurance.

HOW DO we view the trials and testings that come our way? Do we have the kind of attitude that James suggests?

According to our text, trials are tests of faith that are planned by God. They come in all sizes and shapes. In the last chapter we discussed "the charge of the mosquitoes," which are the pesky pressures of daily living. There is no end to the variety! But now let's focus on God's *purpose* in life's trials.

God does *not* desire to squash us like bugs, destroying us. Quite the contrary. He plans and hopes for us to find trials a life-giving experience. Someone has proposed that trials are "God's appointed way forward." And yet, too often we think that afflictions keep us from moving in faith. Stressful situations are designed to purify, strengthen, and develop Godly character. Trials are meant to build patience, faith, and total dependence on God. Testings are God's method of discipline, which enable us to glorify Him and to know Him better. By discovering and studying God's reasons for suffering, we can learn to count it all joy when we find ourselves in difficulties.

"If it weren't for this trial, I would have more time to develop spiritually. I could be devoted to prayer, reading the Bible, serving my church and witnessing to others about what You have done in my life. If it weren't for this obstacle *You* put in my way, I could really live for *You!*" Have you ever thought to say something like this to God? I have. I first saw my unsaved husband as the obstacle to my moving forward. And then he accepted Christ, so I had to blame other trials, often in the form of time pressures and routine inconveniences, for my seemingly restricted progress. The trial *appears* to be the obstacle that's going to prevent us from growing and becoming fruitful. But as we begin to gain God's perspective, it becomes apparent that the trial *is* "God's appointed way forward!"

It would be impossible to exhaust the reasons why God has planned trials and testing in our Christian pilgrimage. But we will appreciate His heart and better understand His purposes if we consider the following eight aspects to "God's appointed way forward" through trials and testing.

1. *Trials and testing are a part of life*. We cry out, "Must there be trials?" Jesus answers affirmatively in Matthew. He assures us that trials and testing *are* a part of life not to be avoided because we are Christians.

> "Therefore everyone who hears these words of Mine, and acts upon them, may be compared to a wise man, who built his house upon the rock. And the rain descended, and the floods came, and the winds blew, and burst against that house; and yet it did not fall, for it had been founded upon the rock. And everyone who hears these words of Mine, and does not act upon them, will be like a foolish man, who built his house upon the sand. And the rain descended, and the floods came, and the winds blew, and burst against that house; and it fell, and great was its fall" (Matthew 7:24-27).

Christ is saying that we *are* going to run into storms. There *will* be rain; there *will* be wind in every life because that's the very nature of this world. The statement infers *when* they come, not if. But He gives us a choice. First, He offers us a solid foundation — Himself and His principles for living victoriously. If we act upon them we will find that our feet are "founded upon a rock" — Jesus — when the storms of life come. On the other hand, if we choose to "go our own way, and do our own thing," not adhering to His teaching, Jesus assures us that our foundation will be self-centered and as unstable as sand. Life will shift, drift, and shatter when the winds and storms hit. And they *will* hit.

While this portion of Scripture points out that testing and trials *are* a part of life, it also raises an important question. What *is* our foundation? Is it Jesus and obedience to Him? A lovely old hymn challenges us with these words: "Be very sure, be very sure, your anchor... grips the Solid Rock! This Rock is Jesus."

2. _Trials and testing are intended to build godly character._ Today many want to be stable, consistent and strong in character, yet these qualities are miserably lacking in our society and in our churches. Perhaps it is because we have resisted learning God's purposes in trials and bypassed His way forward. Patience could be described as fortitude, stability, persistence, adult Christian character and consistent living for Christ. With each trial, the Lord wishes to build character that wasn't there before or reveal His character to others through us. The trial is not meant to shove us backward because the Lord isn't out to produce "backsliders." He's committed to moving us forward toward mature, stable, consistent Godly character.

It has been revealing for me to discover God's interest in developing my character. I always thought I had a fine one. I detected shallowness in others, but failed to see it in myself. From behind rose-colored glasses, I couldn't recognize my quick temper, unchecked words, unkind thoughts or selfish desires.

The Lord has periodically and faithfully shown me areas of my life where I was trusting in my own ability to become God's woman. Sometimes, we treat God like a rubber stamp, insisting on His stamp of approval for our self-sufficient, self-confident, self-willed attitudes. As I walk through "various trials" and face these disgusting disclosures of self, I am reminded that what God wants to work into my life is Christian character — Christ's holy nature.

Going through a time of testing does _not_ in itself build godly character into our lives! Only in accepting His will and appropriating His power will we see Christ's nature prevailing. We have to pass the test! In Romans 8:28 and 29 God assures us that He causes all things, including the tragedy and petty trials of life, to work together for good according to His purpose. His plan is to conform us into the image of His Son. We are partakers of His divine nature (2 Peter 1:4). Both passages point to godly, consistent Christian character — Christ's control rather than shallow self control.

Perhaps you've heard of the sculptor who was asked how he made the beautiful horse from a cold, hard slab of marble. "Simple," he replied, "I just took my chisel and chipped away at everything that didn't look like a horse!" I like that. I picture

God faithfully chipping away at anything that doesn't look like Jesus in our lives. He views the finished product, and smooths our rough edges. When we realize His nature in us is the ultimate goal, we can sing for joy, "Keep chipping, Lord, keep chipping!"

3. *Trials and testing are meant to purify and strengthen us*. Proverbs 17:3 says, "The refining pot is for silver, and the furnace for gold, but the Lord tests hearts." Gold put into a fiery furnace is purified. The fire burns out all the dross, the impurities, the imperfections. What's left is pure, refined, solid gold. That's what testing will do in our lives, if we'll let it. It will purify, strengthen, refine and make us solid.

When someone uses the cliche that we have "a heart of gold," we love it! They are alluding to a pure heart full of goodness. On the other hand, God's Word tells us our hearts are deceitful and desperately wicked. Which opinion *will* we believe?

Let's face it. When we first came to Jesus, none of us had our acts together! We came to Christ knowing that there were areas of our life that needed shaping up. And those who didn't know this had a worse problem — pride. The beautiful thing about the gospel of Jesus is that it invites us to a "come as you are party." None of us had to remodel our lives to be worthy of salvation. We came to Him as we were — needy. Purifying and strengthening is a necessary part of the Christian experience. The Lord has work to do! A friend facing cancer surgery passed this poem on to me. This unknown author said it well:

> He sat by a fire of sevenfold heat,
> As He watched by the precious ore,
> And closer He bent with a searching gaze,
> As He heated it more and more.
>
> He knew He had ore that could stand the test,
> And He wanted the finest gold,
> To mold as a crown for the King to wear,
> Set with gems with price untold.
>
> And the gold grew brighter and yet more bright,
> But our eyes were so filled with tears,
> We saw but the fire, not the Master's hand,
> And questioned with anxious fears.
>
> Yet our gold shone out with a richer glow,
> As it mirrored a form above,
> That was bent o'er the fire, though unseen by us,
> With a look of ineffable love.

Can we think that it pleases His loving heart,
To cause us a moment's pain?
Oh, no but He saw through the present cross,
The bliss of eternal gain.

So He waited there with a watchful eye,
With a love that is strong and sure,
And His gold did not suffer a bit more heat,
Than was needed to make it pure.

4. _Trials and testing develop patience._ Have you ever prayed for patience? I imagine you have. Even before I had a personal relationship with Christ I used to pray. I plastered my ceiling every night with prayers to be a patient mother and wife. Yet, the pressures of motherhood — spilled milk, crumbs, tracked in mud, broken toys, whining and bickering — did not produce a patient mom. The demands of being a wife did not create a joyful, patient companion. In spite of my prayers, confidence hid her face. I lacked confidence that I was making any progress at all in spite of my prayers. The truth of James 1:2, 3 escaped me because the power of the indwelling Christ was not present.

I discovered that becoming a Christian did not produce instant patience either! But it did put me in touch with the Promiser who gives patience as our faith is tried and as we learn to lean on Him. We choose — He provides. We can be either the _short_ — fused, quick-to-anger "reactor" or the trusting, thankful-in-_all_-things "reflector." In each test, trivial or great, we have the choice.

As I drove to a certain church to lecture on this lesson, I praised the Lord that I no longer _have_ to react impatiently to the unexpected trials in life! Jeanne, a friend, met me in the parking lot at 8 a.m. for prayer. We prayed for patience and also for the several hundred women who would soon be arriving. After praying for about an hour we gathered our Bibles and purses, preparing to leave the car. Suddenly, my eyes fell on the headlight switch — pulled to the "on" position. Turning the ignition key confirmed my fear that the battery was dead. This was an unexpected trial — the charge of the mosquitoes! I stood at the pivotal point.

Inside the church, I made a phone call to my husband that would disrupt his well-laid plans for the day. This once volatile and impatient man would be at a turning point himself once I announced my stupidity and reminded him that he had the only AAA card. He would have a forty-five minute drive to get to the church, plus the waiting time and return trip to his desk. There was a lurking fear that I could be called a "flakey, dizzy blonde," (only half in jest) and that the Lordship of Jesus would be over-ruled by our inclinations to react.

The dime clinked into the pay phone. I remembered the Lord's instruction. I *would* consider it all joy. And I would trust the Lord for divinely-imparted patience. It was a cinch I couldn't psyche it up!

"Hello," a serious voice answered.

"Hi, honey! How much do you love me?"

"Oh, I love you enough," his voice seemed to smile.

"Guess what happened?" I asked sheepishly, then quickly recapped the events of a hectic morning.

Dave patiently made the plans to be there by the time the lecture was over. We would not see this problem resolved until after 2:30 in the afternoon, but we would see the joyful reality of patience in our lives as we waited for the battery to recharge.

That morning God answered Jeanne's and my prayers. He revealed the reality of His promise through my simple tale of the dead battery and phone call to my husband. I assured my audience that through this tiny daily trial, God had an opportunity to perform a miracle. There was a time when I would have felt frantic, anxious, defensive, angry and guilty in such a situation. Dave would have reacted with disgusted anger, making *sure* I felt guilty! It was worth the inconvenience for us to see God providing patience as we chose to count it all joy and trust Him with our pesky circumstances.

5. *Trials and testing develop faith and total dependence on Him*. Sometimes it's hard to get our arms around the word *faith*. We know it's something we want, and usually something we feel the need to have more of. But we can't grasp the spiritual meaning of it. We deify faith when we have faith in our faith. The words faith and trust can be interchanged. When God tells us, "The just shall live by faith," He is instructing us to trust in Him. When trials test our faith, the still small voice of God whispers, "Will you please trust *Me* in this?" We are asked to *abide* in His Word, *acknowledge* His promises, *rest* in His assurances, *follow* His leadings, *obey* His commandments, and *yield* to His authority. These are invitations to trust God with our circumstances. *He* is *always* meant to be the object of our trust! That is what total dependence and faith are about—discovering how worthy of our

trust *He* is!

Through trials that are out of control and beyond our power to resolve, the Lord reveals "misplaced trust" (faith in ourselves or faith in our faith) and shows us that total dependence upon *Him* is the *only* way to move forward spiritually. Don't let someone intimidate you by accusing you of using Jesus as "a crutch." His strength revealed in our weaknesses will provide a deep joy that we should not miss.

> "Trust in the Lord with all your heart, and do not lean on your own understanding. In all your ways acknowledge Him, and He will make your paths straight" (Proverbs 3:5, 6).

Remember my telling you about sitting outside the church with my husband, waiting for our car's battery to be recharged? As we waited, patiently enjoying our three hours together, a man walked by with a seeing-eye dog. Just a few feet down the sidewalk, the cement was all torn up, leaving a big hole and piles of dirt. Dave said, "If that isn't an example of faith, I don't know what is."

The man was placing his total dependence and trust in his dog, not knowing what was ahead of him. As we sat and watched, our tendency was to want to cry out an alarm . . . "Look out!" We didn't have as much faith in that dog as he did. But *he* had trust in his dog. No doubt that faith had been tested many times, because he seemed to be confident and patient in responding to the dog's lead. The dog had evidently proved that he was worthy of his trust. As they neared the excavation, the dog steered him off the path, across some grass, down the curb, and into the street. Deftly avoiding traffic, they maneuvered around holes and piles of broken cement and dirt, back to their route.

We're told in Scripture that Jesus loves us, and yet how many of us eagerly respond to His invitation to take His yoke upon us?

> "Come to Me, all who are weary and heavy-laden, and I will give you rest. Take My yoke upon you, and learn from Me, for I am gentle and humble in heart; and You shall find rest for your souls. For My yoke is easy, and My load is light" (Matthew 11:28-30).

That's what we realized as we watched the man walking down the street with his dog. He was *yoked* with his dog by holding onto that bar, and he didn't resist him. He leaned not on his own understanding as he walked from the sidewalk, through grass, off the curb, and into the noisy street. He relaxed and moved with the dog, responding to *his* lead. And that's exactly what Jesus is talking about when He invites us to be yoked with *Him,* to trust *Him* to lead us in, around and through critical, trying circumstances.

We acknowledge with our intellect that God is our loving Father. But until our faith is tested, it will not become a steady conviction. We want to be given strong faith. We like the idea of being protected in a sterile bubble of *joy, patience, peace* and *love* — the fruit of God's Spirit. But we don't pick up on the fact that the Lord *will* develop the fruit of His Spirit — in the crucibles of life, not in a sterile bubble. That blind man's faith was being tested with every step. He was not walking in a bubble, but in a busy, frantic world. In the same way, our faith is tested by every step we take with Jesus.

Having Bible knowledge does not necessarily assure us of spiritual knowledge. We can read the Bible week after week and accumulate much biblical information. But it only becomes spiritual knowledge when we receive life's circumstances as coming from His loving hand, yoked in trust rather than struggle and resistance. The need for total dependence is reinforced, and faith is strengthened in each trial when we say, "Yes, Lord, I will trust only *You,* even in this!"

6. *Trials and testing are part of parental training.* As parents, Dave and I set some guidelines of behavior for our children. When ours are obedient, we encourage them; and when they step "out of line," we warn them to "shape up." It is done in love with the end product in mind — a godly person. Sometimes, when our curly-haired redhead David was just a little tyke, he would *insist* on stepping out of line. Although he knew the guidelines and heard the warning, he willfully chose to disobey. After the disobedience, David and Daddy would march up the stairs into the bedroom, and David would have to lean over the bed with both hands on the mattress to receive his discipline — "whack"! — from an old fraternity paddle.

Children instinctively know they need discipline even though they resist it. There were times when David begged forgiveness before the discipline was enforced. Dave assured him he was loved and forgiven but still proceeded to spank so that David would understand the implications of willful disobedience. It's not enough to say, "I'm sorry," and expect Daddy to back off from the discipline. Once after the "whack" had fallen, David, with a big crocodile tear running down his cheek, sniffed, "Thanks, Dad. I needed that!"

God's Word says that we reap what we sow and disobedience brings discipline plus any other consequences the act might produce. There *are* consequences to our behavior! Our heavenly Father has been faithful to tell us the guidelines that He has set, and He has issued warnings of the consequences for disobedience. Both are repeatedly found, throughout His instruction manual. Like children, we are held accountable.

Our children *know* when they have been disciplined. A firm whack on the bottom when they were young, or going without privileges as teens, has been clearly recognized as discipline. But in the family of God, it seems to be different. Christians will admit to being pruned, purified, tried or attacked, but rarely will they confess that they have been disciplined by God for willful disobedience. Actually, the pruning, purifying, testing, and satanic attacks are all part of child training and are for our good. Sometimes they are deliberately corrective. Occasionally, we all willfully resist God's will. We confess sin but fail to realize that God consistently follows through with discipline. God said about King David's children:

> "If his sons forsake My law, and do not walk in My judgments,
> If they violate My statutes, and do not keep My commandments,
> Then I will visit their transgression with the rod, and their iniquity with stripes.
> But I will not break off My lovingkindness from him, nor deal falsely in My faithfulness.
> My covenant I will not violate, nor will I alter the utterance of My lips" (Psalm 89:30-34).

Do we really think our loving heavenly Father will withhold discipline and not impose upon us the consequences of our disobedience? Are we so proud and so determined to present ourselves as "Mr. and Mrs. Clean" that we can't be honest? Maybe this is why there is so little steadfast, stable, consistent Christian character visible today. We won't be real. There's a bit of Pharisee in us all, which we need to admit and expose. How void our churches are of people who confess their faults to one another according to the admonition to be honest and real in James 5:16. How non-existent is church discipline. How easily we spiritualize our experiences in life, but we fail to face the fact honestly that we *are* being chastened as children whom God loves. If we do not experience chastening from the Lord, we're told we are illegitimate and not in His family at all! Isn't it time we recognize, know and admit when we've been chastened by God? It is part of His perfect plan for our lives! If we prayerfully read this passage, we will become aware of God's faithful, loving parental training:

> And you have forgotten the exhortation which is addressed to you as sons, "My son, do not regard lightly the discipline of the Lord, nor faint when you are reproved by Him; for those whom the Lord loves He disciplines, and He scourges every son whom He receives." It is for discipline that you endure; God deals with you as with sons; for what son is there whom his father does not discipline? But if you are without discipline, of which all have become partakers, then you are illegitimate children and not sons. Furthermore, we had earthly fathers to discipline us, and we respected them; shall we not much rather be subject to the Father of spirits, and live? For they disciplined us for a short time as seemed best to them, but He disciplines us for our good, that we may share His holiness. All discipline for the moment seems not to be joyful, but sorrowful; yet to those who have been trained by it, afterwards it yields the peaceful fruit of righteousness (Hebrews 12:5-11).
>
> Therefore strengthen the hands that are weak and the knees that are feeble, and make straight paths for your feet, so that the limb which is lame may not be put out of joint, but rather be healed. Pursue peace with all men, and the sanctification without which no one will see the Lord. See to it that no one comes short of the grace of God; that no root of bitterness springing up causes trouble, and by it many be defiled (Hebrews 12:12-15).

How can we benefit from the Lord's discipline if we won't recognize and admit it's there? *Every* son receives chastening. By this we share in His holiness. Dare we risk missing revival because of pride that pretends we're without sin, without fault, and therefore without need of chastening? Isn't it interesting that our attitude, once we've confessed sin, is more often in sympathy with the flesh ("I've admitted I was wrong—don't spank!") instead of with the Spirit ("Bring *every* thought into captivity and obedience to Christ!")? To insist on being too good to be chastened, though we admit to trials, is to label ourselves illegitimate.

This is a subject that is a bit frightening to approach. I've seen several church ministries crippled because they wouldn't learn and admit to the Lord's chastening. I've seen God come down hard on friends who wouldn't deal with critical spirits and spiritual pride as the Lord sought to reveal and purge it. And I *know* I've seen my own personal ministry altered and restricted to cause me to acknowledge His discipline and enable me to share His Holiness and the fruit of His righteousness. It has been painful, but growth is evident, as I seek to verbalize the chastening that I recognize in my life.

Parental training is the part of trials and testing that we are least honest about. If we do not accept it, we will have an unrealistic picture of God's character and His dealings with His beloved children. It's time we face this issue. God is *faithful*. We must learn that *He will be as faithful to His warnings as He is to His promises!*

7. *Trials and testing are designed to glorify God.* When a person suffers and demonstrates stable, steadfast, consistent Christian character in his circumstances, it is a testimony to others of God's grace and power, and God is glorified! The ultimate goal of testing is to pass the test. We can go through a trial and be either *bitter* or *better.* If God's glory is our goal, bitter is not the right choice.

For several years, my friend Pat, a leader in our Bible study, has chosen to glorify God in many trials. We stood by her in prayer when a malignant melanoma was removed from her leg. She sparkled as she told us "how good her God was" to give her witnessing opportunities as she trusted Him through her ordeal. God was glorified as she chose to consider it *all* joy.

We prayed for Pat again when a mastectomy was necessary two years later. Once again she radiated and spoke of the "goodness of God" through it *all,* and He was glorified. After that surgery, a mass in her stomach was discovered. And though the operation revealed a benign tumor, it also left an aftermath of severe pain that was almost unbearable. Our Leadership prayer chain was activated repeatedly for several days.

We had house guests at that time who were strangers when they arrived. It was my privilege to entertain them, but a higher priority was to visit Pat. So I put the two needs together and took them with me to the hospital. We entered Pat's room and saw a frail, pain-weary woman sitting helplessly in a chair. The sparkle and quick bounce were missing. Pain was written on every angle of her face, and I wanted to cry.

As we visited, Pat's weak voice shared with this young couple, who were launching into full-time Christian work, how the Lord had worked in her life. The more she spoke of Jesus and of making disciples for Him, the stronger her words became. His goodness, His faithfulness, His sweet love were once more glorified through Pat's pain. And the mixture of sparkle and pain, light and suffering, grace and weakness were overwhelming! His strength *was* made perfect in weakness, just as the Bible says. God was glorified through this precious servant of His, because that is her goal in life—to glorify God.

Our guests have become corresponding friends, and they have assured us repeatedly of their prayers for Pat. They realized that she ministered to them so deeply in the darkest hour of her trial. They knew that she didn't "feel" joyful, but they *saw* that she chose to consider it joy. In the midst of trials, the fruit of His Spirit was reflected in this small, yielded vessel. Pat is now in good health and an even stronger witness to His glory.

Since trials are a part of life, our desire as we go through them should be to glorify God. That goal will transform our attitude into better instead of bitter. Any goal other than this will prove to be self-serving, and we'll find our feet on shifting sand rather than anchored on the solid rock.

8. *Trials and testing are the path to knowing God better!* Knowing is a certainty—something we can count on, a word of hope because it contains a promise from God. As His children, we say that we *know* God is our loving Heavenly Father. But it is through the tests of faith that our child-like statement becomes a steady conviction! Facing a martyr's death, after a lifetime of triumphant service laced with trials, the apostle Paul proclaimed, "For this reason I also suffer these things, but I am not ashamed; for I know whom I have believed and am convinced that He is able to guard what I have entrusted to Him until that day" (2 Timothy 1:12).

We're told in Romans 1:17, "The righteous man shall live by faith." When our faith has been tested and His Word has been tried, and both have proven true, our faith becomes confident, steady conviction. Our faith is not in our faith, but in God who has repeatedly revealed Himself true to His Word. That takes time. It is part of growing to maturity in Christ. But it is well worth the persevering.

Dozens of situations reconfirm His faithfulness to a trusting heart. When God proves faithful in a situation, it is easier to trust Him the next time. Why? Because we've gotten to *know* Him better.

We need to *know* God's character and that His purposes toward us are good. We discover the description of His character in the Scriptures, but we see the reality of His character in our trials. God was not a liar when He said, "For I know the plans that I have for you," declares the Lord, "plans for welfare and not for calamity to give you a future and a hope" (Jeremiah 29:11). My friend, Dr. Bill Bright, has stated it more simply in the *Four Spiritual Laws:* "God loves you and offers a wonderful plan for your life."

We must *know* that the Lord is sovereign. He has not carelessly let situations encompass us that were never part of His intended will. He has not lost control! Knowing this, regardless of our circumstances, produces patience.

We must know that the Lord knows us. God explains that He knew us in our mother's womb. He knows our thoughts before they find expression, and He knows our ways. He is omniscient; He knows all.

He is also omnipresent which means He is always with us. Strange isn't it, how we can lock Him out of our thoughts and hearts, and yet in reality we cannot escape His presence or being on His mind? Psalm 139 allows us to know these truths intellectually, but before we *experientially* know them with joyful conviction, we must have our faith tested. Then we have assurance that He's in control; He's good; He knows me, and He's with me.

Shame on us when we think God has fallen asleep at the controls or that His timing is off! Shame on us when we think that He's made a mistake, that He's failing us and exercising bad judgment! Shame on us when we think we're misunderstood by Him! When we think He's forsaken us, we deny everything He declares, and our faith becomes unbelief. The Lord will continue to design and permit trials until we learn to take Him at His word... to know He is who He says He is and will do what He says He will do. Why does He persist? Because He really wants us to know Him better!

Trials and tests are the way to know God better, because they put us in the position to discover the reality of what He has said about Himself in the Scriptures. The Scriptures reveal Him; the trials prove Him. Acts 17:24, 25 declares that He is on the throne and reigns supreme:

> "The God who made the world and all things in it, since He is Lord of heaven and earth, does not dwell in temples made with hands; neither is He served by human hands, as though He needed anything, since He Himself gives to all life and breath and all things."

He created us and gave us life. Everything we have is a gift from Him. We cannot draw our next breath without His permission.

Other passages reveal God's compassion, love and kindness. The prophet Isaiah wrote:

> Like a shepherd He will tend His flock, in His arm He will gather the lambs, and carry them in His bosom; He will gently lead the nursing ewes.
>
> Who has measured the waters in the hollow of His hand, and marked off the heavens by the span, and calculated the dust of the earth by the measure, and weighed the mountains in a balance, and the hills in a pair of scales?
>
> Who has directed the Spirit of the Lord, or as His counselor has informed Him?
>
> With whom did He consult and who gave Him understanding? And who taught Him in the path of justice and taught Him knowledge, and informed Him of the way of understanding?
>
> Behold, the nations are like a drop from a bucket, and are regarded as a speck of dust on the scales; behold, He lifts up the islands like fine dust (Isaiah 40:11-15).

As king and creator of the universe, God did not need our advice. He is mighty enough to create all, and tender enough to care about each of us in every detail. "Lift up your eyes on high and see who has created these stars" (Isaiah 40:26). The Lord wants us to understand these things about Him so we can truly know Him better.

I have not attempted to discuss or even fully list the different characteristics of God's character. Many authors have expounded beautifully on this subject and it will be well worth your time to read *Knowing God* by J. I. Packer or *Knowledge of the Holy* by A. W. Tozer. A study booklet called *Behold Your God* by M. Alexander and published by Zondervan is sure to bless your heart. I'm convinced that when we become engulfed with our trials and begin to flounder spiritually, it is because we have lost sight of some aspect of the character of God!

We have looked at eight aspects to "God's appointed way forward" through trials and testing.

Reflect and Act

You may desire to reflect further on what God has shown you through personal experiences and Scriptures.

Trials and testing are:

1. Part of life.
What was the last trial you experienced that tested your faith in God?

2. Intended to build godly character.
How did you "reflect" God in a way that you wouldn't have, were it not for His indwelling Spirit?

Did you "react" and reveal self?

What did God's Word reveal?

3. Meant to purify and strengthen us.
If you reflected God's Spirit within, how were you spiritually strengthened?

If you reacted, revealing self, what sin did you confess to be cleansed and purified?

Did you claim 1 John 1:9?

What did God's Word reveal?

4. Used to develop patience.
Describe a situation in which you consciously chose to consider it *all* joy, knowing patience would result.

Describe choosing unbelief and what you experienced instead of patience.

5. Intended to develop faith and total dependence on Him.
In the situation described in 1, how was your faith in God affected?

What did you learn about your dependence on Him?

What did God's Word reveal?

6. Part of parental training.
Describe a situation where God disciplined you for disobedience in order that He might train you.

What did God's Word reveal?

7. Designed to glorify God.
Describe how God was glorified, or not glorified, as a result of your responses to the above trials.

What did God's Word reveal?

8. The path to knowing God better.
How did experiencing these trials give you better knowledge of your heavenly Father?

What did God's Word reveal?

After honestly analyzing your trials and your responses to them, this prayer may help you voice your desires to the Father:

Father, forgive me when I try to squirm out of the trials of life. I know You have wise and good purposes in all You plan for me.

Forgive me for the times I have resisted Your yoke when rest to my soul was promised. Help me to be joyfully expectant about the abundant life and adventure that can be found even in trials.

Thank You for building godly character into my life. Purify and strengthen me. Give me divine patience. I want to be better, not bitter. Develop my faith and teach me to lean on You in total dependence.

Sometimes it hurts, but thank You for spanking me. Help me to have as much faith in Your warnings as I have in Your promises. Do what You must to glorify Yourself through my life! I am eager to draw near to You and to know You better. Amen.

Chapter 3

Handling Life-Shattering Crises
James 1:4

4 And let endurance have *its* perfect result, that you may
be perfect and complete, lacking in nothing.

WE'RE ALL interested in experiencing what it is to lack nothing,
aren't we? But in order to achieve this, we must first heed the
warning and understand the condition.

"Letting," a close cousin to waiting, is the key to lacking
nothing. Letting is no kin at all to emotional "whining," when
we claim His patience through testing and then ask to be
delivered...*now!* "Letting" is an act of our will and proves patience has been given by God.

We're missing the point when we cry out to God for immediate deliverance from our trials. As we studied the nature of
trials and testing we saw that *through* them we will know God
better. Yet in our prayers for deliverance we choose to keep our
distance and remain strangers to magnificent truths about
God, — His trustworthiness, the depths of His sufficiency and
love, the wisdom of His timing and the results of His refining.
How foolish and how lacking in true patience we are. Our impatience wants to hurry God's hand! We don't like waiting! And
"letting" involves waiting.

The Lord has imperishable nuggets of truth to show us *in*
trials. Oswald Chambers once remarked that he could probably
fit the amount of grace he had experienced during *good* times
on the face of a penny. But the grace of God he sensed in periods
of sorrow, pain and grief was incalculable! I'm sure He did not
make that sort of statement as a glib, poetic thought, but as a

tested truth. Christians' testimonies of the reality of God's love, grace and sufficiency, almost always are made in the context of a time of testing, aren't they?

Whether it is "the charge of the elephant" (a life-shattering crisis) or "the charge of the mosquitoes" (pesky, trivial traumas of daily life, usually arriving in swarms), the Lord assures us that the outcome will be prosperity, abundant provision — no lack if we'll only "*let* endurance have its perfect result." In other words, if we *keep* counting it all joy, *wait* on God's timing, and don't squirm out of patiently walking *through* "God's appointed way forward," we will possess the rich reward. We will be perfect and entire, *lacking* nothing.

All of this would seem unfathomable were it not that our God has made sure that we're in excellent company. He has surrounded us with examples of those who have *let* endurance have its perfect result. The Scriptures reveal many who learned letting and gave up whining for immediate deliverance. They also reveal those such as Sarah who became impatient and took things into their own hands and reaped the consequences. Also, Christian biographies and the testimony of godly friends have encouraged us as we've seen them lack nothing as they've "let patience have her perfect work" during "the charge of the elephant" or "the charge of the mosquitoes."

Lacking nothing can be a reality. Several friends in Scripture and in personal situations have taught me letting and have proven that what God promised is true.

The Bible offers examples of many who did not respond with pleas for quick release when faced with trouble.

Poor Shadrach, Meshach and Abed-nego. Their story is recorded in Daniel 3. In Babylonian captivity, they lived under the yoke of a government strange to them. Yet, when their friend, Daniel, was appointed ruler over the whole province of Babylon, ·he appointed them to positions of influence. Because of their authority and high visibility, they soon became "sitting ducks."

King Nebuchadnezzar made an image of gold, and required all to worship it or be cast into the midst of a fiery furnace. Daniel's three friends would not bow to the image, and were brought before the angry king.

Now here's where regarding it all joy and "letting" usually break down. Wouldn't we expect to see Shadrach, Meshach and Abed-nego on their knees whining, "Oh please, God, deliver us now! . . . from this wicked king and his fiery furnace"?

Instead these men stood on the "rock" and testified that their God was certainly able to deliver them. They added that even if God chose not to, they had no intention of serving false gods and worshipping golden images!

Bravo! They stood for their faith! Now enter God, who dramatically delivers them for their noble witness! Right? Wrong! The facts of their deliverance begin with verse 19:

> Then Nebuchadnezzar was filled with wrath, and his facial expression was altered toward Shadrach, Meshach and Abed-nego. He answered by giving orders to heat the furnace seven times more than it was usually heated.
>
> And he commanded certain valiant warriors who were in his army to tie up Shadrach, Meshach and Abed-nego, in order to cast them into the furnace of blazing fire.
>
> Then these men were tied up in their trousers, their coats, their caps and their other clothes, and were cast into the midst of the furnace of blazing fire.
>
> For this reason, because the king's command was urgent and the furnace had been made extremely hot, the flame of the fire slew those men who carried up Shadrach, Meshach and Abed-nego.
>
> But these three men, Shadrach, Meshach and Abed-nego, fell into the midst of the furnace of blazing fire still tied up (Daniel 3:19-23).

This was the picture of despair. They may have reckoned it all joy to stand their ground for worshipping God. And they may have determined to "*Let* endurance have its *perfect* result." They were willing to become history in a trail of smoke as they were ushered into heaven.

However, God did not choose to let them be martyred. Let's look further and observe the lessons in the familiar story.

> Then Nebuchadnezzar the king was astounded and stood up in haste; he responded and said to his high officials, "Was it not three men we cast bound into the midst of the fire?" They answered and said to the king, "Certainly, O king."
>
> He answered and said, "Look! I see four men loosed and walking about in the midst of the fire without harm, and the appearance of the fourth is like a son of the gods!" (Daniel 3:24, 25)

In shock, the king ordered the Hebrew men out. Addressing them as "servants of the Most High God," he marveled that they had survived. Their hair wasn't singed, nor did they even smell of smoke. The mighty king astounded the realm with a new decree.

> "Blessed be the God of Shadrach, Meshach, and Abed-nego, who has sent His angel and delivered His servants who put their trust in Him, violating the king's command, and yielded up their bodies so as not to serve or worship any god except their own God.
>
> "Therefore, I make a decree that any people, nation or tongue that speaks anything offensive against the God of Shadrach, Meshach and Abed-nego shall be torn limb from limb and their houses reduced to a rubbish heap, inasmuch as there is no other god who is able to deliver in this way."
>
> Then the king caused Shadrach, Meshach and Abed-nego to prosper in the province of Babylon (Daniel 3:28-30).

Now, doesn't that beat all? These men chose to withstand "the charge of the elephant" and "*let* endurance have its perfect result." In their deliverance, God was glorified and they were promoted, lacking nothing.

Many Christians have faced similar persecutions. Some were martyred. Chet Bitterman, a young man with Wycliffe Bible Translators in South America, was kidnapped recently, held hostage and finally murdered. But Chet was delivered from his fiery trial lacking nothing . . . "for to be absent from the body is to be face to face with the Lord" . . . and He is everything!

The point is not whether our deliverance is accomplished in this side or in the other side of death. The point is whether *we see the Lord in the furnace.* Our three friends in Babylon did and so did the king who put them there. Reports indicate that while Mr. Bitterman was "letting endurance have its perfect result," he told his captors about Jesus repeatedly. He saw and declared the Lord *in* his furnace. The last chapter is not written in his captors' lives. Perhaps they'll see the Lord in the furnace they created for that godly man and acknowledge Him.

For some, deliverance comes instantly. For others, freedom comes after enduring for several years. After one of my lectures on letting which explains how Shadrach, Meshach and Abed-nego saw the Lord *in* their fiery trial, a member of a Bible class came to me. She opened her Bible to one of the blank pages where she had drawn the illustration I used that morning on the overhead transparency.

Violette spoke of the comfort and strength she had received as the reality of Christ being with her *in* her fiery trials had dawned increasingly upon her. While Shadrach, Meshach and Abed-nego apparently found deliverance on the same day that they entered the furnace, Violette had been left *in* her furnace for several *years!* And yet, she was strengthened and she grew visibly as she came to know that the Lord was with her *in* her unavoidable trials. Vi has been in the process of learning to deem it all joy and letting endurance have its perfect result. She has permitted me to relate excerpts from her story:

> Since I lacked the beauty and talents others had, I was timid, fearful and insecure about facing life. I always felt totally inadequate. Fortunately, I married a wonderful person who had a dynamic, cheerful personality, high standards and intelligence. He was the leader upon whom I leaned during our 34-year marriage.
>
> The nearest I came to having to accomplish anything on my own was in raising our three sons. The oldest is mentally ill with schizophrenia. I always felt I'd handled him poorly and caused his illness. I felt bewildered, frightened, shattered, betrayed and forgotten by God with this baffling problem which I couldn't solve. A desperate inward longing for help turned into acute, constant chest pains which lasted many years.
>
> In addition, I had a slipped disc in my lower spine for which I had been doing exercise for a long time. If there were ways to handle physical stress, I reasoned, there must also be ways to handle spiritual stress.
>
> Because of my tragic sufferings, it was difficult for me to see God as protective and loving. Either He wasn't loving at all, or He just didn't love me.
>
> Then one day, I heard that single word . . . *grace.* It fascinated me. Was it really possible to experience it? This brought a hope which urged me to keep searching.
>
> After a Bible study class the teacher explained the good news of Jesus Christ in a very simple way to me. Although I knew of my great inadequacies, I never thought of myself as a willful, "miserable sinner." Yet, when I understood that it meant being separated from God, putting myself and my desires on the throne of my life instead of putting God in charge, I realized I had usurped His power, which was sin.
>
> In my mind and heart something vital had clicked into place, like the missing piece of a jigsaw puzzle. I invited

Jesus into my heart. That was the turning point. Within a few days my severe chest pains completely disappeared.

There have been many ups and downs in my spiritual walk, but I am slowly learning to let go of my fears and anxieties, and allow God's grace to fill my heart. My worries lessened to the degree where the family could joke about it. In fact, my husband nick-named me "the Desperate Duck."

For the next three years, I was in the furnace of trials. I nursed my husband through terminal cancer. Then my mother, who lived with me also through terminal cancer. My oldest son had to be put in the mental hospital, and I lost my only sister to cancer.

The Lord removed my guilt about being a poor mother. He enabled me to deal more effectively with my losses, and He gave me a new family of Christian sisters who showed love and support.

I have a drawing from a dear friend in the front of my Bible. It's a picture of a tearful little girl standing in the midst of life's fiery trials. But she is also smiling, because standing next to her with His arm around her, is Jesus. No matter what the problems are, Jesus is always the answer. I realize that God's ways are beyond my understanding, but He said, "Lo, I am with you alway" and — "My grace is sufficient for thee: for my strength is made perfect in weakness" (Matthew 28:20 and 2 Corinthians 12:9 KJV).

Vi has ministered to me as I've watched the Lord refine and test her life — producing pure, solid gold. Grace — the word that caught Vi's attention — is very evidently being supplied to this dear child of God.

We learn "letting" by observing the examples of others. The book of Daniel reveals evidence of that process. I don't know where Daniel was when his three friends were tossed into the furnace, but since he arranged their jobs in the first place and they were "brethren," you can be sure he heard of their deliverance and promotion.

How powerful their God must have seemed as they reflected on the sequence of events. How full of faith their hearts must have been, having seen first-hand God's ability to do "exceeding abundantly beyond all that we ask or think . . . " (Ephesians 3:20). They were already men of faith, but you can be sure that they emerged from their fiery trial with a greater God!

Daniel not only witnessed the deliverance of his friends; he watched the trial and redemption of King Nebuchadnezzar. Seeing the Lord in the fiery furnace had caused the king to *acknowledge* the power of God to overrule and deliver. But he still needed a humble heart. God gave the king a vision, which Daniel interpreted, and then brought it to pass. The king became like a beast of the field, eating grass like an ox, to learn the supremacy of God in world rulership. Daniel 4:25, 26 says he would suffer like that "until you recognize that the Most High is ruler over the realm of mankind, and bestows it on whomever He wishes . . . you [shall] recognize that it is Heaven that rules."

Because Daniel was willing to speak God's word boldly, King Nebuchadnezzar survived *his* fiery trial with the faith to proclaim:

"But at the end of that period I, Nebuchadnezzar, raised
my eyes toward heaven, and my reason returned to me, and
I blessed the Most High and praised and honored Him who
lives forever;
For His dominion is an everlasting dominion,
And His kingdom endures from generation to generation"
(Daniel 4:34).

Daniel, through his witness of the king's trial, knew an even *greater* God! he saw a man humbled completely and then restored to power...lacking nothing.

Belshazzar, the King's grandson, failed to remember Nebuchadnezzar's trial and defiled the temple's vessels by drinking from them during a feast. As he and his wives "praised the gods of gold and silver, of bronze, iron, wood, and stone" (Daniel 5:4), handwriting appeared on the wall announcing the destruction of his kingdom and the end of his life. When his astrologers and soothsayers could not read the writing, his wife suggested he call on Daniel "in whom is a spirit of the holy gods" (verse 11). She reminded him that illumination, insight and wisdom were found in Daniel's dealing with King Nebuchadnezzar.

So once again, Daniel was called upon to "tell it like it is." He reminded King Belshazzar of all that Nebuchadnezzar had been through . . . how "his spirit became so proud that he behaved arrogantly" (verse 20) . . . how "his heart was made like that of beasts . . . until he recognized that the Most High God is ruler over the realm of mankind" (verse 21). He rebuked this king, reminding him that though he *knew* all those things, he had not humbled his *own* heart, but had chosen to worship idols. God used Daniel to tell him that the handwriting on the wall meant his kingdom was finished. God was ready to remove that king. That night he was slain and God's Word was proven true.

Daniel continued to "let enduring have its perfect result," as he served under yet another ruler, King Darius, the Mede. The king recognized a leader when he saw one and appointed Daniel as one of three presidents who, for the ruling of the people, had one hundred and twenty princes accountable to them. In this chain of command, Daniel held quite an impressive position, and the king was even thinking of setting him over the entire realm.

Something interesting happens when the teacher has a "pet" or the king has a "favorite." Colleagues become envious and treacherous. The other two presidents and the one hundred and twenty princes couldn't catch him in a fault or in being unfaithful in his service. So using as bait his worship of God, they set a snare. They approached King Darius, appealing to his pride saying,

> "All the commissioners of the kingdom, the prefects and the satraps, the high officials and the governors have consulted together that the king should establish a statute and enforce an injunction that anyone who makes a petition to any god or man besides you, O king, for thirty days, shall be cast into the lions' den" (Daniel 6:7).

Their statement was a lie. I'm sure they hadn't consulted Daniel! The king signed the unalterable decree, and the power struggle was in motion.

Daniel could have avoided a head-on confrontation by simply not praying for thirty days. Sounds tempting, doesn't it? Daniel chose instead to worship God, to "consider it all joy" and "let endurance have its perfect result," rather than whine for quick deliverance from this test of his faith. How do we know? Daniel 6:10 tells us:

> Now when Daniel knew that the document was signed, he entered his house (now in his roof chamber he had windows open toward Jerusalem); and he continued kneeling on his knees three times a day, praying and giving thanks before his God, as he had been doing previously.

His treacherous enemies turned him in promptly, reminding

the king of his edict. We see in verse 14 that King Darius was distressed about it.

> Then, as soon as the king heard this statement, he was deeply distressed and set his mind on delivering Daniel; and even until sunset he kept exerting himself to rescue him.

His heart was sickened as he acknowledged his helplessness to deliver Daniel. But he knew that the law could not be changed. As a man of character, he must remain true to his word.

> Then the king gave orders, and Daniel was brought in and cast into the lions' den. The king spoke and said to Daniel, "Your God whom you constantly serve will Himself deliver you" (verse 16).

By faith, the king spoke of God's ability to shield and deliver. As he spent a sleepless night fasting, I'm sure both the king and Daniel had time to draw upon God's word, such as the absolutes recorded in Samuel:

> "As for God, His way is perfect; the word of the Lord is tried: He is a buckler to all them that trust in Him. For who is God, save the Lord? and who is a rock, save our God? God is my strength and power: and He maketh my way perfect" (2 Samuel 22:31-33 KJV).

We read that God *did* shield Daniel from the mouths of the lions, bringing him forth unharmed. Those who plotted against him, along with their families, were thrown to the same lions. Before they reached the bottom of the den, the beasts attacked and crushed all their bones. What a sad illustration of "reaping what we sow" that turned out to be! Daniel's endurance produced its perfect result in the announcement of the king:

> Then Darius the king wrote to all the peoples, nations, and men of every language who were living in all the land: "May your peace abound! I make a decree that in all the dominion of my kingdom men are to fear and tremble before the God of Daniel;
> For He is the living God and enduring forever,
> And His kingdom is one which will not be destroyed,
> And His dominion will be forever.
> He delivers and rescues and performs signs and wonders
> In heaven and on earth,

Who has also delivered Daniel from the power of the lions" (Daniel 6:25-27).

The concluding verse of that chapter explains that Daniel withstood "the charge of the elephant" and prospered during that king's reign. God was a *shield* as he trusted Him. In every trial Daniel had come through "perfect and complete," *"lacking in nothing"*! Daniel never lived a life of ease, but by his choices he demonstrated an admirable godly character.

Similarly, my friend Cindy made an honorable choice and was given deliverance from a turbulent situation. I watched this woman discover cancer, undergo a mastectomy, and then stand up at a coffee shining like a sunbeam to explain the reality of Jesus being with her through it all.

Cindy was young, beautiful, the wife of a successful businessman and the mother of young children. As I listened to what she was saying and looked at the radiance in her eyes, one sure thought crossed my mind . . . "No one can psyche that attitude up!" I had seen nobility, a "stiff upper lip" and "the power of positive thinking" demonstrated by others as they faced calamity. But I had never seen anyone radiantly focus on another person like Cindy did – Jesus and His love, His power, and His presence – with such total abandonment in the face of crisis. God used this woman in a special way to draw me irresistibly to my Savior.

As time passed, Cindy and I enjoyed growing together spiritually. Soon another "charge of the elephant" came against her. The doctors had told her that she should have no more children because a pregnancy could stimulate cancer activity. When Cindy found herself pregnant, she consulted with her doctor. The latest school of thought was that a pregnancy might not present a danger after all. After her husband asked the doctor what *he* would do if it were *his* wife in this situation, the doctor admitted he would still have a clinical abortion. That settled it. Jeff didn't want to take any chances with his wife's health.

But Cindy resisted and refused. She argued that she could not believe that her heavenly Father would permit life to be planted in her body so they could willfully destroy it. Over a period of time, tensions flared as he demanded the abortion to protect her well-being. Their relationship suffered as a time factor added to the mounting pressure. Cindy's dilemma was intense.

How could she submit to her husband's decision for abortion and blatently deny God's will to bear a new life?

In desperation because she lacked joy, patience and peace, she went to a wise Christian woman for counsel. By the time she went, she already knew in her heart what she would hear. After hearing her tearful anguish, the dear friend answered, "I don't know where in the Bible it says we should or should not have an abortion when health may be in jeopardy. But I do know that we are to submit to our husbands, as unto the Lord, in *everything*. When we do what the Lord instructs, thanking Him and trusting Him with our circumstances, He has promised to lead and shield us." "I knew you'd say that," Cindy acknowledged softly.

Returning home, she asked her husband's forgiveness, and confessed her willingness to submit to his leadership, knowing he was trying to be wise in protecting her life. Now here's where we would expect God's deliverance, isn't it? She's quit resisting, so her husband will certainly change his mind. Not so. He appreciated her willingness to understand his decision and promptly called the doctor to schedule the surgery.

Now Cindy's joy, patience, peace and long-suffering returned. All attempts to manipulate her husband had failed miserably. She made her move in willful response to what she knew was in God's Word. She would now trust God's will to be done, even though the strength of her original conviction had not altered. Her struggle had ceased. The battle *was* the Lord's. Her husband was no longer "the enemy," but her friend who was acting according to all the light he had. Cindy was "letting endurance have its perfect result."

By this time a few of us knew of this situation and were standing by in prayer. My prayers were basically for God's grace to be sufficient for Cindy. That seemed like a nice, safe prayer since I knew the Lord had already promised that His grace *is* sufficient. Can you imagine my amazement when I received word that while Cindy was packing to go to the hospital, she experienced abdominal pain and had a miscarriage in the privacy of her home?

God had stopped the mouth of the lion! He was a shield to the one who trusted Him! God *does* make our way perfect! We all emerged from this situation with a bigger God and Cindy, through "letting," was *lacking in nothing*. She learned the harmony of submitting to her husband's leadership while seeing the protective shield that God provided for her well being.

Another friend, Betty, struggled painfully through this lesson. During a telephone call, Betty explained that her husband had been forced to quit drinking because of poor health. Since she had recently become a Christian, she also desired to quit drinking. But her husband demanded that she continue, and ordered milk for himself and an Old Fashioned for her whenever they dined in public. He insisted that she drink it, reordering drinks several times before their food was served.

Betty admitted this had been going on for months. She always resisted, argued and cried for mercy, sometimes causing heated scenes. But her resistance made him more determined to dominate the situation. She often became physically ill from the liquor.

This particular evening she was to meet him at their Country Club where they would be entertaining one of his clients and his wife. She had called to ask me what she should do.

Leaning on my own understanding, I wondered why her husband's bitter heart desired to destroy her. And yet I knew God's Word desires us to submit to our husbands, as unto the Lord, in everything—*even when he's wrong!* Although many people try to make exceptions to what this verse in Ephesians 5 teaches, it *says* in everything! So I reminded Betty of that first, telling her about my friend Cindy. Reviewing God's promise to be "*a shield* to those who take refuge in Him" (Proverbs 30:5), we also confessed "casting our cares on the Lord," "considering it *all* joy" and "giving thanks in *everything.*"

I quickly told Betty that she could not walk in my faith or in Cindy's, but she could be encouraged by and learn from examples. She had to decide if *she* could commit this situation to the Lord and trust Him with *her* circumstances. I advised her to pray and purpose in her heart to submit to her husband rather than quarreling and whining and pleading. In this way she would step out of the way, giving God room to work on her behalf. After a brief prayer, we hung up.

How I prayed that Betty would count it all joy and choose to "let endurance have its perfect result" so that she could see God's deliverance! In a way I felt like King Darius. My hands were tied. I could not go with her and deliver her from the mouth of the lion. I could only claim God's promises, knowing His character was at stake.

A few days later, a letter from Betty arrived with a book. Betty wrote that she had met her husband and the other couple at the club. True to form, her husband ordered milk for himself, an Old Fashioned for her, and drinks for the other couple. She didn't argue or resist. Her husband continued to order round after round of drinks. My heart sank and my mind raced as I imagined the suspenseful scene. "Lord, what happened?"

Quickly, I read on... he ordered round after round of drinks for the other couple never noticing that she had not taken a sip of her first drink. The waiter removed her untouched glass as the meal was served at 10:30 p.m. without comment from the others. She was hungry, but she was sober! And Betty knew that the living God *is* "a shield to all of them that trust in him."

The book she mailed to me was a study on resisting Satan. As I read it, I meditated on 1 Peter 5:7-9:

> "Casting all your anxiety upon Him, because He cares for you. Be of sober spirit, be on the alert. Your adversary, the devil, prowls about like a roaring lion, seeking someone to devour. But resist him, firm in your faith, knowing that the same experiences of suffering are being accomplished by your brethren who are in the world."

Betty's choice to cast her care on the Lord and be steadfast in her faith, helped her resist *the devil*. She had been resisting the wrong foe. Her husband needed her love and prayers, not her resistance. Once she chose to "*let* endurance have its perfect result," she was delivered out of Satan's trap.

So many couples seem to have mistaken the enemy! How often the devil grabs a victory that should have been the Lord's, because an individual resists a mate and drives a wedge into a relationship that God sees as "one flesh." We create division where God designed unity.

The situations that Cindy and Betty went through dealt with their willingness to submit to their mates. One thing is important to remember. We are *not* submissive if we choose when or when not to submit, depending on what we think or feel. With that attitude, the individual is still very much in control.

This is not an issue of wives and husbands alone. Ephesians 5 instructs those filled with the Spirit to submit themselves one to another. This condition is a reflection of the heart that is yielded obediently to God. People who strive against the idea of submitting to any authority, who decide when or when not to obey God, are usurping God's leadership. God is not Lord—they are.

Although God was on the throne of her life, Carole's marriage did not survive the "charge of the elephant." With her daughter Susan, she helplessly watched a mid-life crisis attack her home and family. Her husband gradually faded from his Bible study. Soon a curly perm, a gold necklace and a sports car expanded his deflated self-image. Finally, he confessed there was another woman and initiated the divorce. I watched and prayed through one and one-half years of agony as this family was shattered. Not day by day, but moment by moment this Christian woman and her daughter had to choose to trust the Lord with their circumstances. Week after week as we talked or quietly worshipped in church, I saw them "letting" God control the situation. Heartsick, Carole kept the door open to reconciliation until the courts slammed it shut. Although miracles happen, fervent prayer hasn't yet seemed to keep this man from willfully resisting God. But I'm assured of one thing. This mother and daughter have "let" God consistently work through their trial, and they know His faithfulness.

Obedience to God's Word is required even when we cannot understand the reasons for death and tragedy. Kenny was only 9, but he was in heaven after suffering with a brain tumor for more than a year. His white-haired grandfather spoke at the memorial service, held at our children's Christian school where Kenny's father coaches. He could not answer the question of why he still lived when this young boy was gone, but this heart-broken man's face beamed with joy as he reaffirmed faith in his sovereign God by declaring with Job: "The Lord gave and the Lord has taken away. Blessed be the name of the Lord" (Job 1:21). With the pains of grief evident, a godly family chose to "consider it all joy". . . "letting endurance have its perfect result." I know God is not about to let them down now. They shall be "perfect and complete, lacking in nothing"!

Others have faced death with equal courage and endurance. Regretfully, Alice learned that her daughter's first baby was mongoloid. Amid the emotions, heartache, and concerns the Lord provided many witnesses to the special blessing these children can be to the heart that accepts them as gifts from God. Several days after hearing the news, I called Alice. "Dianne," she informed me, "I told my precious daughter that she must trust in the Lord one day at a time and that God told us to 'be anxious for nothing!'" Those words might have sounded glib and hollow coming from me, the Bible teacher. But they packed a wallop coming from a tender-hearted mom who would soon be sharing in her family's adjustment to a special grandchild's death.

We've looked at the deliverance of Shadrach, Meshach and Abed-nego and Violette's companionship with Jesus in her ongoing fires. We've reflected how Daniel observed the trials of others and triumphed when he too was tested. And we've seen how God continues to shield those who trust Him — in Cindy and Betty, Kenny's family, Carole and her daughter and Alice and her family. Each faced "the charge of the elephant," and saw God in their circumstances. And each emerged from the trials with a greater understanding of God.

Let's look again at our verse, with a few added comments to tie down the significance of "letting." "And let endurance have its perfect result." Endurance or patience is a fruit of the Spirit, so we know that its work is perfect. "That you may be perfect and complete, lacking in nothing." God's ultimate purpose for us is the abundant life He offers, in spite of our circumstances. When we face tests His way and pass them, we lack nothing. When we flee, we flunk the tests and we are empty — lacking all He intended. If we fail, He can lovingly recycle us into His perfect way forward.

Notice the order of these first four verses:
1. *Faith* exists.
2. It is *tested* through trials.
3. Passing the test produces *endurance.*
4. Extended patience ("letting") results in *lacking nothing.*

We often want to start with number 1 and jump to number 4, avoiding "the charge of the elephant." But God's Word reveals the process of testing and "letting" as the path to His ultimate purpose . . . *lacking nothing.* Oh, that we would willingly walk the path in His yoke by simply "letting!"

Reflect and Act

You may wish to examine your progress through these steps by completing the following thoughts:

The last time I experienced the "charge of the elephants" was

My reaction to the situation was

Because I (did, did not) allow endurance to have its perfect result, the outcome was

Chapter 4

Asking for God's Wisdom
James 1:5-8

5 But if any of you lacks wisdom, let him ask of God, who gives to all men generously and without reproach, and it will be given to him. 6 But let him ask in faith without any doubting, for the one who doubts is like the surf of the sea driven and tossed by the wind. 7 For let not that man expect that he will receive anything from the Lord, 8 *being* a double-minded man, unstable in all his ways.

WE HAD lived in Columbus three years, when one day Dave took my hand to pray over lunch. After blessing the food he added, "I sense that we have fulfilled our purpose here in Columbus, Lord. If you have another place for us to go, please direct us. Give us your wisdom. Amen." My heart flooded with peace as Dave prayed. I knew it was time to move and that the Lord was leading my husband.

Minutes after Dave's prayer, the telephone rang. "Dave, this is Paul. Are you ready to go overseas to serve the Lord?" The national director of our organization was at the airport passing through and had paused to call. As Dave explained his prayer and the timing of Paul's call, we moved rapidly from peace to expectancy.

The weeks passed, and we petitioned daily for God's wisdom in this matter. I claimed the promise of Proverbs 16:3, "Commit your works to the Lord, and your plans will be established." We asked for the treasure of God's wisdom and then waited.

Sitting still and waiting is the hardest test of faith we have to go through. We desperately want to break the silence and make something happen. Several months passed since that prayer over lunch. Often I would turn to James and reread verse 5 for reassurance and strength.

God's wisdom is more precious than gold. It is not like man's wisdom. The Apostle Paul reminds us of this difference which he explained to the Corinthians:

> Let no man deceive himself. If any man among you thinks that he is wise in this age, let him become foolish that he may become wise.
> For the wisdom of this world is foolishness before God. For it is written, "He is the one who catches the wise in their craftiness"; and again, "The Lord knows the reasonings of the wise, that they are useless" (1 Corinthians 3:18-20).

A truly wise person possesses biblical knowledge and uses it to make decisions which glorify God. Plugging into the right power source enables us to tap the resources of Heaven. Our needs are met according to His riches in glory in Christ Jesus (Philippians 4:19).

Because He knows our desperate need for His divine provision, He will not send any of us away empty-handed. I will never hear him remark, "Dianne, are you back again? More wisdom? You dumb little kid. What did you do with the supply I gave you yesterday?" I was to learn the availability of God's wisdom through some of the really tough decisions facing us.

As James states the condition in verse 5, "*If* any of you lack . . ." Praying regularly for wisdom requires humility. "I am a very capable person" is denied as we admit lack and humbly ask. God's Word tells us *He* knows the way. "He leads us in paths of righteousness. . ." We were designed to follow Him, so what do we need? We need the wisdom to detect His ways. So what do we do? ALL too often, we "go to the phone, not the throne"! We quickly turn to family, friends, colleagues, neighbors or mates to seek solutions *before* we ask God for wisdom. If we don't ask for widom from God *first,* how will we recognize Godly advice when it *is* spoken through human instruments? On the other hand, if we know we lack wisdom in a specific situation and we ask of God *first,* we *will* have the discernment to recognize Godly council, and God's Spirit will check our "sloppy thinking" when it occurs.

God's wisdom seemed to be with Dave and me as we considered our alternatives. Though we had talked seriously with ministry heads in Africa, Asia and Europe, it soon seemed evident that our move would be within the States. Scriptures, the counsel of friends, and the desires of our hearts all pointed to a position in Washington, D.C. As we planned our exploratory trip to Washington, we were invited unexpectedly to talk with some people in Philadelphia who had developed a ministry to executives. We obliged happily, not wanting to miss God's will. Uprooting the children would be a big step, and we didn't want to make a mistake.

The five-month wait to discover the right location was a joyful time of "letting" and experiencing supernatural patience. During that time, when I was tempted to wonder about God's wisdom, I read the warning in James:

> But let him ask in faith without any doubting, for the one who doubts is like the surf of the sea driven and tossed by the wind. For let not that man expect that he will receive anything from the Lord, being a double-minded man, unstable in all his ways (James 1:6-8).

We can't ask in faith and then cross our fingers. Unbelief is always sin and will block the answer. Wavering faith equals withheld wisdom. And wondering is wavering. Too often we verbalize:

"Lord, look at this mess!"

"Where are You in this situation?"

"I'm confused."

"Have You given me Your wisdom, or haven't You?"

"Of course You have."

"Haven't You?"

"But Lord, what if . . . ?"

Such instability in character and conduct will affect every area of life. Unsteady faith in God will produce inconsistency in how we relate to others, how we discipline children, control emotions, submit to authority, maintain moral values and accept responsibility. Failure to receive is the result when the "carnal thinking" believer vacillates in faith. Let not that man expect that he will receive anything from the Lord.

This two-faced approach toward God is a struggle which wastes time and energy. When my faith is fluctuating concerning God's wisdom in a situation, I am so distressed that I can barely dress and make the bed. It's demotivating, depressing and disastrous to live in unbelief — wondering if God really means what He says. But the Word teaches, "Whatever is not from faith is sin" (Romans 14:23).

One minute we may admit our need, ask for wisdom and believe for the answers. We stand firm with Paul acknowledging, "Now to Him who is able to do exceeding abundantly beyond all that we ask or think, according to the power that works within us" (Ephesians 3:20). The next moment, when the elephants and mosquitoes charge mercilessly and instant solutions do not appear, we panic. Our minds are driven and tossed by a sea of doubt which submerges joy and shipwrecks patience.

Doubts seemed nonexistent as we returned from our successful ten-day trip to Washington. The moving instructions were now clear. The Lord was definitely calling us to make a contribution to the ministry developing on Capitol Hill. We couldn't wait to arrive home and call back our acceptance to join our colleagues there.

God's timing was perfect! On the way home, we stopped for a meal to celebrate our fifteenth wedding anniversary. As we waited for our dinner to be served, Dave pulled out a small ring box and handed it to me across the candlelit table.

"Honey, this is to replace the old cracked one," he declared.

Inside the velvet box a lovely gold band reminded me of our new life and the marriage Christ had saved. We had our special assignment from the Lord—our beginning. It was all so romantic and exciting. A new ring, a new assignment, a new beginning!

That evening, after we arrived home, a young couple dropped by to visit. I eagerly recapped for them much of the last five months' wait and our plans to move. As we visited with our guests, the telephone rang. Dave was gone a long time, and when he returned, he stated simply, "I guess we won't be going to Washington. Honey, we're moving to Philadelphia."

This unexpected "charge of the elephant" knocked the wind out of me. I was stunned. How or when our guests left that night I couldn't say. I only remember that I cried for three days. Hot flashes of anger alternated with cold chills of pity. How could Dave make this stupid decision without me after we had discussed it and prayed together for five long months? We were being forced out of God's will by an unreasonable man who wanted Dave to submit to his authority.

In calmer moments, I reminded myself that God was sovereign. Obviously, He was guiding Dave and his superior as they sought His will. Even though I was disgusted with Dave's joy and peace in the matter, I knew I must submit to his choice. But I couldn't! Who did this director think he was—shoving us around like pawns? No, Lord, I won't accept it. My feelings continued throwing temper tantrums.

After the third sleepless night I arose at 5 a.m. and asked Dave's permission to call Ann, the woman who had discipled me and given me a love for God's Word. She and Ralph were among friends who had felt that Washington was the place for us. Surely, she would sympathize and agree that men had knocked us out of God's perfect will.

Nervously, I dialed her number and was relieved that she was so kind about being awakened early. "Ann," I sputtered and cried, "God just isn't in control anymore." Tearfully, I relived five months of waiting, emphasizing the events of the last five days. I quoted Scripture to convince her *and* myself that I knew I was to submit and consider it all joy. Bouncing from faith to distress over our problem, I finally stopped to catch my breath.

At that moment God gave Ann a one-liner that became the turning point in my trial. "Honey," she answered, "You know the Word, and you know you must choose to obey and trust in our sovereign Lord. You just may have to wait for your emotions to catch up with your choice." While I was being tossed like the waves of the sea, God had established her thoughts. I felt like the disciples during the storm on the Sea of Galilee who woke the Savior, crying, "Master, Master, we are perishing!" And being aroused, He rebuked the wind and surging waves, and they stopped, and it became calm. And He said to them, "Where is your faith?" (Luke 8:24, 25).

Silence allowed His supernatural calm to flood my consciousness. "Ann," I spoke softly, "Thank you. I love you for saying what I needed to hear." After hanging up the phone, I slipped to my knees in prayer, confessing unbelief and being two-faced with God through wavering. "Lord," I prayed, "I confess the misery I've experienced without Your peace and joy. Forgive me for my obstinate ways. I desire to yield my will to Your wisdom and to Dave, the spiritual leader You've given me. Amen." The storm had passed.

From time to time I may waver and sputter, but through testing I've seen my convictions strengthened. The Lord *is* in everything. He has not lost control. He does work it all together for good to those who love Him and His purposes.

Twenty-eight days after our fifteenth wedding anniversary we moved to Philadelphia, believing that divine wisdom had sent us there. Five years of victorious service for God have been the result.

Through such trials, I have learned that human wisdom and godly wisdom *are* directly opposed to one another. Often Christians take God's Word and twist it to fit *their* will. They rationalize to get their own way and do not care that God's wisdom is missing. But God wants us to transcend our human intellect and natural resources and see our need for spiritual guidance. The wisdom God offers goes beyond secular knowledge.

In Christ we are new creations — spiritual beings whose minds are enfused with His divine creativity. "For who has known the mind of the Lord, that he should instruct Him? But we have the mind of Christ" (1 Corinthians 2:16). He wants us to be an influence in our homes, occupations, ministry and relationships, because we have His thoughts. When we capture this concept, even the mundane, daily tasks take on added meaning.

If we desire spiritual wisdom in the midst of trials, faith must depend on the power of God to reveal the resources for deliverance. Productive faith trusts the Provider and receives His provision via heavenly wisdom. Paul revealed to us that faith in secular wisdom is not God's intended plan. "And my message and my preaching were not in persuasive words of wisdom, but in demonstration of the Spirit and of power, that your faith should not rest on the wisdom of men, but on the power of God" (1 Corinthians 2:4-5). God's wisdom included God's power to deliver from any and all circumstances.

Asking for wisdom, believing it will be provided, and waiting for the answer will lead to immediate or eventual deliverance from trouble. We're struggling unnecessarily if we're too proud to ask or if we ask and then waver. Pride and unbelief are devastating to the Christian.

When Godly wisdom is present, happiness and peace will be evident in the life of the believer. Solomon recognized the value of wisdom when he wrote:

> How blessed is the man who finds wisdom,
> And the man who gains understanding.
> For its profit is better than the profit of silver,

And its gain than fine gold.
She is more precious than jewels;
And nothing you desire compares with her.
Long life is in her right hand;
In her left hand are riches and honor.
Her ways are pleasant ways,
And all her paths are peace.
She is a tree of life to those who take hold of her,
And happy are all who hold her fast (Proverbs 3:13-18).

God has provided the way to happiness, blessing and release from trials.

Reflect and Act

Review with me the steps to receiving God's wisdom and the hindrances to avoid.

1. If we lack, godly wisdom is available.
2. Wisdom comes by asking.
3. God refuses no one and gives to all men generously.
4. Ask in faith without wavering.
5. Believe patiently without doubting.
6. Doubting produces instability.
7. Instability equals withheld wisdom.
8. Productive faith plus godly wisdom equals deliverance.

If you need immediate help, pray this prayer to begin your release from the trial you are in:

Father, I come to You with unmixed devotion, wanting nothing but to be in Your will. Cleanse me of any unbelief or pride that would toss me about like the waves of the sea. Give me a clean heart and fill me with Your Spirit. I ask for supernatural wisdom, that I might be guided by Your creative, liberating power. Help me to see man's wisdom as You see it and to treasure Your wisdom as gold. Amen.

Evaluate your relationship with God and reliance on His resources by considering the following:

1. It seems I can trust God to direct me and give me wisdom in many areas, but there is a weak spot where I waver between belief and unbelief. It is

2. The last time I asked God for wisdom was

3. God's provision came in the form of

4. I was hindered from receiving God's resources by

Chapter 5

The Joy of Being
Rich or Poor
James 1:9-12

9 But let the brother of humble circumstances glory in his high position; 10 and *let* the rich man *glory* in his humiliation, because like flowering grass he will pass away. 11 For the sun rises with a scorching wind, and withers the grass; and its flower falls off, and the beauty of its appearance is destroyed; so too the rich man in the midst of his pursuits will fade away.

12 Blessed is a man who perseveres under trial; for once he has been approved, he will receive the crown of life, which *the Lord* has promised to those who love Him.

WHEN IS a person poor? Is it when his income falls below Washington's official poverty level? Is it when someone has only one meal a day, and sometimes misses that?

On the other hand, when is a person rich? Do three cars in the driveway make a family rich? Is it finally getting out of an apartment into your own home?

In chapter 1, verses 9 to 11, James reminds us that neither poverty nor riches can be measured by these standards. The passing-awayness of this world's symbols of wealth make a totally new criteria necessary. Both the poor and the rich must realize that this world's things self-destruct, but that their relationship with God *is eternal.*

James focuses first on the person considered poor by this world's standards. He is to rejoice in his exaltation. Why? Because he has been exalted by God. He is an heir with Jesus Christ to all eternal blessings (Romans 8:17). The Lord supplies all his needs — spiritual, emotional and physical (Philippians 4:19). According to Jesus, he need not be anxious about food, drink or clothing (Matthew 6:25).

If you have ever met a poor person who loves and trusts Jesus, you've seen a radiant glow reflecting his moment-by-moment fellowship with God. He is free from the crippling struggle to survive and from the fetters that so easily bind a man of means. He can live above the tendency to get anxious over making ends meet, feeding his family, and finding security in a job. He has confidence in the promises of God's Word to sustain the exalted, chosen child of God. The poor man who looks at life through God's Word wisely sees that his station in life isn't really what matters! With divine perspective, he can rejoice obediently, knowing he is exalted in this life and forever.

In contrast, the rich person is described by James with greater emphasis.

By the world's standards, most of us would be rich indeed. We're products of a materialistic society and manage to enjoy many of its comforts. Some of us may actually be living well beyond our means, spending every penny plus some with plastic charge plates — leaving us with enough debts to make us feel poor. But by worldly standards we live exceptionally well!

The rich man's tendency is to get entangled in more and more and more of this world's goods. He has the money to purchase many things, but never has quite enough to satisfy his insatiable appetite. It's easy to have a lovely home but want a bigger one; have a pretty car but want a newer one; like last year's wardrobe but want the latest fashion; wish we had ordered something else on the menu, or planned a bigger and better trip in the midst of the one we're supposed to be enjoying — never quite satisfied.

Many of us fall into that trap. I certainly have. Those desires became my measuring stick for security, success and happiness; but the more I had, the emptier my heart became. Scripture tells us that our heart is where our money is invested. Mine was locked up in our home, social life, club life, trips — in everything we could do to spend money on ourselves!

James, looking at this with divine perspective, reminds us that the rich man should evaluate his possessions realistically. In verse eleven he compares his wealth to grass. It's beautiful, green and flourishing; but when the sun rises and time passes it will become parched, and it will wither and die. How better to say, "You can't take it with you." The day is coming when we'll have to do without it. Either our money will pass away through financial reverses or inflation or we will die. At best, riches can provide only temporary fulfillment. The man of God who is rich is humbled when he recognizes what is worthy of his rejoicing — his relationship with God. He couldn't buy it or earn it. He knows he doesn't deserve it — and he knows it has eternal value.

The cross of Jesus Christ is truly the great leveler! Here the poor are exalted and the rich are made low. We stand at the foot of the cross equal in Christ — saved sinners. As Jeremiah points out, riches are nothing to boast of.

> Thus says the Lord, "Let not a wise man boast of his wisdom, and let not the mighty man boast of his might, let not a rich man boast of his riches; but let him who boasts boast of this, that he understands and knows Me, that I am the Lord who exercises lovingkindness, justice, and righteousness on earth; for I delight in these things," declares the Lord (Jeremiah 9:23, 24).

Man's wisdom, might and riches can be definite distractions when we are trying to make decisions in God's will.

My husband's law practice was flourishing. He had invested in quite a bit of real estate. (He called it playing Monopoly — no hotels on Park Avenue or Boardwalk, but lots of little houses around the board!) We had just moved into the dream house I had designed and we had had built on seven acres — when God called Dave to a full-time Christian ministry. My prayer as a baby Christian had been, "Here am I, Lord — send me!" But the reality of it happening caused some initial "wavering."

Was it really God's will for Dave to lay aside all of his training in the field of law (his wisdom), quit the climb up the success ladder (his riches), lay aside his position as a partner in a law firm (his might) and launch out in a faith venture serving Jesus Christ? The verse above brought me over that hump (though it took a year to call myself a missionary!), and it has been sheer joy serving our King.

Because "the laborer is worthy of his hire," we had the humbling task of developing a support team, the financial and prayer base for our work. We believed we were called by God to do His work and that God's children would share eternally in the rewards of that work through their faithful investments. Paul wrote "for even in Thessalonica you sent a gift more than once for my needs. Not that I seek the gift itself, but I seek for the profit which increases to your account" (Philippians 4:16, 17).

One couple who stepped forward to invest in our work was a black family who lived in the inner-city with their seven children. We lived on different economic and social levels, but we all loved Jesus. For the last nine years we have stood together at the cross — yoked with this couple in Christ's service. We know that their faithful investment of five dollars every month has equal value in God's sight with anything He may have accomplished through us.

Riches don't always have to be money. If you're over 30, there's a good chance you've stood in front of a mirror sadly contemplating a few pouches, dimples or wrinkles. The cosmetic industry, health spas, and sports centers stash away millions of dollars each year as vanity drives many to seek perpetual youth and to prove that the mirror and God's Word are wrong! But whether we like it or not, we're all drying up and withering away! It is pathetic to see men and women frantically try to hang on to the riches of their youth, when the mirror clearly tells them that youth is fading away! Whether our "riches" are money, beauty, health, position or power, we're still "here today and gone tomorrow." No one has beat the system yet!

One exciting way to look at the inevitability of the aging process is to develop a sensitivity to the beauty and character in wrinkles and graying hair. Each passing day brings us one day closer to being face to face with Jesus. Try that thought on for size! It always makes my heart smile.

Youth, looks, and life styles are passing qualities, so why not "hold loosely the things of this world" and invest our lives in things of eternal value? In Matthew 6:19-24, Jesus clearly urges this approach when he tells us to lay up treasures in heaven. In the eternal realm we aren't fighting a losing battle.

Whether rich or poor, we'll be content with our station in life if we'll practice two things — giving and enjoying, in that order.

Giving sets the stage for us to rejoice. God used King David to teach his people to give to the Lord's work. The result of their giving was their joyful response. "Then the people rejoiced because they had offered so willingly " (1 Chronicles 29:9).

David continued to declare something that we lose sight of too often, causing us to become possessive and stingy:

"Both riches and honor come from Thee, and Thou dost rule over all, and in Thy hand is power and might; and it lies in Thy hand to make great, and to strengthen everyone. Now therefore, our God, we thank Thee, and praise Thy glorious name. But who am I and who are my people that we should be able to offer as generously as this? For all things come from Thee, and from Thy hand we have given Thee" (1 Chronicles 29:12-14).

It is easy to hold on to or misuse our gifts from God. By selfish indulging we can destroy our health. By feeding on "garbage," our minds can become polluted and corrupted and, by being possessive with our money, we can become enmeshed with "things" while our lives go to pieces right before our eyes! In the process of grabbing and "holding on," we become selfish and empty. These are harsh words. For everyone who insists they are not naturally that way, let me remind them that the Bible says they are.

In addition to giving, God wants us to enjoy our possessions. If we will let King David's people serve as models to teach us to give willingly, we'll discover not only the joy of giving, but the freedom of "holding loosely" and really enjoying what we have left. God blessed many in the Scriptures with the wealth to give and have plenty left to enjoy, but they maintained an attitude of love for God, not money. They enjoyed the things their riches provided, and at the same time loved and trusted the Provider.

Paul passed this principle on to Timothy — "Instruct those who are rich in this present world not to be conceited or to fix their hope on the uncertainty of riches, but on God, who richly supplies us with all things to enjoy" (1 Timothy 6:17).

It's easy to subtly reverse giving and enjoying and find ourselves "holding on" rather than "holding loosely." We learned the difference while driving one summer between Pennsylvania and Colorado. As we headed west, we stopped in Columbus where old friends gathered with us over lunch to enjoy a reunion. As we prepared to leave, the hostess slipped a twenty dollar bill into my hand explaining, "The Lord has led me to give you this. You'll undoubtedly have needs arise as you travel." We had prayed for an extra twenty dollars to buy some much needed stainless steel flatware for the kitchen, but I instantly felt this money was not an answer to that prayer. As I tried to explain to Mary that I didn't feel this was intended for me—she only insisted she mustn't be denied the joy of giving. So after thanking them, we continued on.

It would have been easy to enjoy looking forward to purchasing that flatware, which was on sale in Philadelphia, but the thought persisted: This is not meant for you to enjoy, but to give. Luke 6:38 loomed in my mind.

> "Give, and it will be given to you; good measure, pressed down, shaken together, running over, they will pour into your lap. For by your standard of measure it will be measured to you in return."

Apparently the Lord had something to teach us about first giving, then enjoying. The money was tucked away in a side pocket of my wallet where it wouldn't "slip through my fingers," and it was offered to the Lord's will in prayer.

Two nights later, after a long day driving through Kansas, we were eager to find our motel and rest. It was dusk, about eight in the evening, when we spotted a car off the road with the hood up. As we passed, we noticed that the young black motorist had his wife and baby in the car. We were in the middle of nowhere! We realized we were passing a neighbor in distress and turned around.

As we pulled up behind their car, I remembered the lawyer who questioned Jesus about his neighbor, and the Lord answered with the parable of the Good Samaritan who encountered the troubled traveler on his journey.

After talking with the couple, we discovered they were "family"— having known Jesus for three years. Eventually we managed to tow this weary group to a service station twenty minutes down the road. The women and children stayed in the station while the men tried futilely to revive a "dead car." As the station attendant, who was also a new Christian, called home to ask his wife if they could put up the travelers for the night, it was easy to part with the twenty dollar bill. They resisted like I had, until I explained the prayer of commitment to give it rather than enjoy it. Of course, the true enjoyment was found in the giving.

By midnight our weary bodies fell into the bed at the motel. As we lay quietly unwinding and reflecting on the unusual events of the last few hours, David's intense little voice flooded the room from his overflowing, ten-year old heart — "Gee, this has been the most exciting night of my life!" We wouldn't have gone quite that far — but we were all happy and content as we went to sleep.

The next day on the road, I discovered two little envelopes that had been tucked into my Bible at the luncheon in Columbus. Both notes were full of love and contained fifty dollars in cash. Wow! The Lord meant Luke 6:38 when He said it! Why are we always amazed? We reviewed the events thus far and agreed to keep giving to see how the Lord might continue to use us.

During our stay in Colorado, we invited a couple to dinner that we supported in Africa. Learning that their pay check had been short, it was easy to part with the fifty. Afterward, yet another envelope containing money turned up mysteriously in my purse. Suffice it to say that we saw several hundred dollars pass through our hands during that trip. It truly is more blessed to give willingly than to receive. We learned that dramatically as a family. There's "high adventure" in traveling with the Lord!

The four-day trip from Colorado to Philadelphia ended as we pulled in the driveway on Lawson Avenue, chiming in unison, "It's good to be home!" As I waded through five weeks of mail, our lesson came to an end. A lady in Indiana wrote asking if we would take the enclosed gift of twenty dollars and use it to buy something for our kitchen. It was time to enjoy!

> Blessed is a man who perseveres under trial; for once he
> has been approved, he will receive the crown of life, which
> the Lord has promised to those who love Him (James 1:12).

Blessed means *happy*. Why do we associate happiness with a life of ease — a dream world seen through rose-colored glasses? Happiness is not sitting at a resort with a good tan, good food and good clothes. We've all seen people with those things who are perfectly miserable. God says the happy person is the one who endures temptation and passes the test. And what is the reward? The crown of life.

A man is happy who endures and overcomes the temptation to grumble and complain, live in unbelief, rely on his own wisdom and be discontent with his station in life. Why? Because he's learned to consider it all joy, patiently let God's timing unfold, ask for divine wisdom and rejoice.

Verse 12 in the first chapter of James ties down the 11 verses that have preceded it. Assuredly, we will be tested in our reaction to outward trials, in our choice to draw on God's wisdom or man's and in our response to our poverty or wealth. Verse 12 challenges us to endure, and endurance pays off! How could we resist God's promise of happiness and the crown of life?

Reflect and Act·

Check yourself with the following to see if your response to poverty or wealth is in line with what God teaches:

1. Describe the circumstances when you last gave something willingly.

2. Explain the result of your giving. Did you rejoice because of it?

3. Identify something that God has recently given you simply to enjoy.

4. What things in your life do you need to hold more loosely? Or what is *yours,* that you haven't given to God?

Chapter 6

The Key to Overcoming
James 1:13-17

> 13 Let no one say when he is tempted, "I am being tempted by God"; for God cannot be tempted by evil, and He Himself does not tempt anyone. 14 But each one is tempted when he is carried away and enticed by his own lust. 15 Then when lust has conceived, it gives birth to sin; and when sin is accomplished, it brings forth death. 16 Do not be deceived, my beloved brethren. 17 Every good thing bestowed and every perfect gift is from above, coming down from the Father of lights, with whom there is no variation, or shifting shadow.

DOES GOD ever tempt us? We often act like He does by thanking Him when things go right, but blaming Him when things go wrong. James will make us think twice before we accuse God again of tempting us to sin.

The word "tempted" is used interchangeably in Scripture with "tried" or "tested." The trial is a refining process that is meant to test, purify, and strengthen our faith. There are only a few places in Scripture—and this is one of them—where tempting refers to "prompting one to sin." This is something God will *never* do. Instead He points the finger at our own lust. He doesn't even let us off the hook with the cliche, "the devil made me do it." We are clearly said to be drawn away and enticed by *our own lust!*

The word "lust" usually conjures up the meaning of illicit sensual or sexual longing, which certainly is a serious problem. But we cannot confine our definition to that. Lust simply means "desire." Not all things we desire are sexual, sensual or, for that matter, even evil—initially. John gives us a clearer picture of the nature of lust:

> Do not love the world, nor the things in the world. If anyone loves the world, the love of the Father is not in him.

For all that is in the world, the lust of the flesh and the lust of the eyes and the boastful pride of life, is not from the Father, but is from the world. And the world is passing away, and also its lusts; but the one who does the will of God abides forever (1 John 2:15-17).

According to this Scripture, there are three areas of lust which encompass "all that is in the world." First is the lust of the flesh, the desire for things that please our bodies, our appetites, ourselves. One of the things I love most is a handful of cookies. Normally, there's nothing evil about a cookie. There are times I'll pray about my diet, asking for God's help, and then spend several hours thinking about cookies. Finally, I'll walk into the kitchen, knowing there is no such thing as *one* cookie for me. When I eventually reach in the drawer, I may end up eating a dozen at one time. I have been enticed and drawn by my own lust. The desire to satisfy my flesh has become an action that borders on gluttony.

It is these "pets" in our lives that we pamper, ponder, and satisfy instead of enforcing godly discipline. Is it our wardrobe? Nutrition? Jogging? In themselves they are good, but they can become the *source* of our satisfaction in life. The desire to satisfy our flesh can entice us away from our wish to see Jesus be Lord of all.

In addition to being tempted by these innocent "pets," we can't avoid worldly temptation toward sexual immorality, drinking, drugs, erotic music and pornography. Constantly, we're being bombarded through television, music, literature, theater and art. Unless checked supernaturally, we will do what comes naturally and be drawn into sin by *our own lust*.

The second inward snare which James mentions is the lust of the eyes. At some time we all have wanted another's home, job, well-behaved children or mate. The lust of the eyes means desiring what we see. It is to look at something and say, "I want it!" This is the internal sin of coveting. The temptation leads to external sin when we figure out a way to get the object and fulfill our desire. People will steal, lie, cheat, even kill, to get what they want — if they crave it badly enough.

The third area of lust is the pride of life. God will never tempt us to be high-minded, haughty and arrogant. The pride of life is opposite to the abundant life that Christ offers. As the following passage describes, pride has been a hindering part of man's nature.

There is a kind of man who curses his father,
And does not bless his mother [rebellious pride].
There is a kind who is pure in his own eyes,
Yet is not washed from his filthiness [self-righteousness].
There is a kind — oh how lofty are his eyes!
And his eyelids are raised in arrogance [vain pride]
(Proverbs 30:11-13).

Does this sound like a twentieth century news clipping describing current times? No, it is the divinely imparted wisdom of Solomon transcending the ages.

Although lust is a serious problem for a believer, temptation to lust is not sin. Jesus was tempted in all areas, but never sinned.

James' analysis of temptation in verse 15 shows us how lust may result in spiritual death: "Then when lust has conceived" shows that lust is first a thought. If the initial idea is not resisted but entertained, "it gives birth to sin." And "when sin is accomplished," it can erupt into external action. If it does, it "brings forth death" which is severed fellowship with God.

All our habits are formed by this progressive pattern outlined in God's Word. First, we conceive the idea, and it becomes a desire. After holding the desire for a while, which is internal sin, we allow that desire to become an action. Once we've committed the sin, it becomes easier to do a second time — a third — and a fourth. Somewhere along the way that repetitive action becomes a habit. And before we know it, the habit has become imbedded in our character. Because we are no longer able to control our desire, a habit has formed which cannot easily be broken.

Many of us have found ourselves in that situation. As a young woman, I went through this kind of process with many things — one of them being alcohol. In my teens, I was drawn and enticed by lust.

In the lust of my flesh, I desired to drink something that could alter the way I felt and behaved.

In the lust of my eyes, I wanted to appear sophisticated at 15, so I drank.

In the pride of life, I was just as "cool" as my peers, and was going to prove it!

First the thought came, then a cherished desire, followed by an external action. I gagged when I drank at first, but it became easier each time. Before long, a habit had a grip on me, often producing several hang-overs a week. I felt like the individual described in the Book of Proverbs:

> . . . Who has redness of eyes?
> Those who linger long over wine,
> Those who go to taste mixed wine.
> . . . And you will be like one who lies down in the middle
> of the sea,
> Or like one who lies down on the top of a mast.
> ". . . I will seek another drink" (Proverbs 23:29-35).

After I'd known Christ personally for more than a year, the habit was broken.

In addition to luring us into unhealthy habits, temptation often affects our relationships with people. At first we are tempted to sin in our thought processes. We might be persuaded to have an ungodly reaction to or attitude toward a person. Dwelling on that thought can become an internal sin that erupts into word or deed. Gradually, our attitude and actions toward that person become a habit. We are in bondage every time we even *think* of that person!

Because temptation to sin is subtle, the Lord warns us in James 1:16, "Do not be deceived, my beloved brethren." It's easy to rationalize, so be careful. Don't let your temptations entrap and deceive you!

So the instruction in James is clear. Lust is desire of the flesh. Through lust, the flesh, eyes and pride are stimulated to acts of sin. There is a progression from thought to habit that renders spiritual death—our "separation" from God's fellowship and His overcoming power. This lesson explains the warning not to err. Sadly the person who lets temptations lead to sin is never satisfied!

In Proverbs 30 where we saw the vivid descriptions of rebellious, self-righteous and vain pride, there is also, in verse 16, a list of four things that are never satisfied:

> 1. "Sheol" (the grave) will always call more to itself. The grave is a picture of death and carnality. We're never satisfied when we are carnally minded!
> 2. "The barren womb" is a picture of the God-shaped vacuum in our hearts that Pascal said could only be filled by God and not any created thing. The emptiness described requires spiritual rebirth and the constant filling of the Holy Spirit.

3. "Earth that is never satisfied with water" connotes a dry, parched wilderness. Sin and death never leave us filled, fruitful and flourishing, but dry and dissatisfied.

4. "And fire that never says, 'Enough'" becomes an image of sin that consumes and destroys. It is out of control and must be fed to continue burning.

Like the grave, the barren womb, the parched earth and fire, lust and sin in their various forms are never satisfied! To be in bondage to them is to be the prisoner of a tyrant with an insatiable appetite.

How then do we overcome lust? If our own lust is the problem, deliverance will not come until we call a spade a spade. Our own desires have us imprisoned and we need a deliverer. After we repent and acknowledge the cleansing blood of Jesus, we are ready to claim the promise of God's provision. God will provide a way out of the temptation. He has said so in His Word.

> Therefore let him who thinks he stands take heed lest he fall. No temptation has overtaken you but such as is common to man; and God is faithful, who will not allow you to be tempted beyond what you are able, but with the temptation will provide the way of escape also, that you may be able to endure it (1 Corinthians 10:12-13).

If there's an area in our lives where we're in bondage, we must admit it and confess it as *sin*. God's Word is truth! If we haven't been delivered from sin, the problem is that we haven't reached the place where we can't bear it. We'll never plead for His way of escape until we've truly come to the end of our excuses, our rationalizing, and our own attempts to resolve the problem. The question is not whether God means business with us, but whether we mean business with Him!

In the past I've let my fetish for "cookies" remain somewhat of a joke as I've excused an extra ten pounds I've hauled around for two years. While the weight bothers me almost daily, it has not reached the point where I can't bear it or I would have sought and obtained God's way of escape. Oh, yes, I've prayed about it! But I'm too quick to rationalize about the occupational hazard of dinners and luncheons being part of my work. Many people let similar pressures keep them in bondage to alcohol or drugs. Who do we think we're kidding?

A humorous attitude doesn't solve the problem either. I can

remember laughing at jokes about drunks when I had a drinking problem. It was easy to jest concerning marriage, while carefully camouflaging a failing one. And now my son and I plaster the refrigerator door with "Miss Piggy" cartoons. He's even made me a snout out of a jar lid. But our humor under duress does not provide deliverance — only tolerance and a camouflage.

Once we come to the end of our excuses and get as tired of our half-hearted prayers as the Lord is, we are in a position to see God work. At first it may require repenting of our sin or desire many times a day. That *can* be exhausting. But I've seen perseverance and the blood of Jesus cleanse from sin according to 1 John 1:7. If we'll hold to the Lord's plan until we see His powerful deliverance, it will be worth it.

God's way of escape is promised in 1 Corinthians 10. In 2 Corinthians Paul said that persevering prayer plays a part in that release.

> For the weapons of our warfare are not of the flesh, but divinely powerful for the destruction of fortresses. We are destroying speculations and every lofty thing raised up against the knowledge of God, and we are taking every thought captive to the obedience of Christ (2 Corinthians 10:4, 5).

Deliverance will come from God as we destroy our speculations, our pride and our lust. When our wandering thoughts are brought "into captivity" to the obedience of Christ, we will not only see redemption established but discernment given. Oh, how we need to do this as temptations continue to bombard us!

When we pray sincerely, God is able to set us free from temptation, lust and sin. The key to overcoming lust is realizing "His strength is made perfect in weakness!" We can then rejoice with the hymn writer:

> He breaks the power of cancelled sin
> He sets the *prisoner free,*
> His blood can make *the vilest clean*
> His blood availed for *me!* From *"O For a Thousand*
> *Tongues to Sing"* by Charles Wesley.)

Now I confess that my cookie capers have become a clever way of cloaking fat. I've been convicted by my own preaching, just as Paul was by his.

Do you not know that those who run in a race all run, but only one receives the prize? Run in such a way that you may win.

And everyone who competes in the games exercises self-control in all things. *They then do it to receive a perishable wreath, but we an imperishable.* Therefore I run in such a way, as not without aim; I box in such a way, as not beating the air; but I buffet my body and make it my slave, lest possibly, after I have preached to others, I myself should be disqualified (1 Corinthians 9:24-27).

Chuck Swindoll, in one of his Insights for Living Bible Study booklets, wisely commented on Paul's words saying, "I get the distinct impression that he feared the age-old problem of trafficking in unlived truth . . . of not taking God seriously." This present author is disgusted with her own rationalizing and has claimed 1 Corinthians 10:12-13! I've asked the Lord never to let me get away with being a phony! I expect to be delivered from these ten extra pounds because of *His* promise and provision.

Reflect and Act

We have learned from James that sin is caused by our own lust. We can't blame God, our mate, or our in-laws for it. The temptation started with our desire and has produced sin, death and bondage. Are we bearing the sin? Are we still rationalizing our problem? Or are we ready to do business with God by claiming 1 Corinthians 10:12-13? No half-hearted prayers of commitment will do. If you are ready to pray seriously for your deliverance, it may help if you will thoughtfully write your prayer in the space provided here:

Chapter 7

The Path To Maturity
James 1:18-21

18 In the exercise of His will He brought us forth by the word of truth, so that we might be, as it were, the first fruits among His creatures.

19 *This* you know, my beloved brethren. But let everyone be quick to hear, slow to speak *and* slow to anger; 20 for the anger of man does not achieve the righteousness of God. 21 Therefore putting aside all filthiness and *all* that remains of wickedness, in humility receive the word implanted, which is able to save your souls.

AFTER DENYING that God can do us any harm by tempting us to sin, James moves on to assert that God does us only good. Temptation to sin does not come from God. Jesus was the good and perfect gift of God. He came from the Father of lights, the immutable, never-changing God, to declare Himself the light of the world. He died that we might be born again to become the light of the world, reflecting His life in us.

God initiates our relationship with Him to reveal His perfect goodness. Scripture teaches that "In the exercise of His will He brought us forth" (James 1:18). In John 6:44 Jesus confirmed, "No one can come to Me, unless the Father who sent Me draws him." James declares in 1:18, "He brought us forth by the word of truth." Peter emphasizes that we "have been born again not of seed which is perishable but imperishable, that is, through the living and abiding word of God" (1 Peter 1:23). Even faith that brought salvation came "from hearing, and hearing by the word of Christ" (Romans 10:17).

In the parable of the sower Jesus explained that the seed was the word of God. According to 1 Peter, it is clear enough that the corruptible seed refers to physical birth and a life that ages and dies. The incorruptible seed relates to the eternal word of God that is planted in a heart and springs forth producing new and eternal life—first fruits to live forever!

Many of us have children that look like us or our mate. We ourselves often resemble a parent or relative. Isn't it amazing that like begets like! More wonderful than this is that we are all human beings! We were not begotten by cats or dogs or other species of creation. We have been procreated by other human beings.

The Bible speaks of a physical birth and a spiritual birth. In the Old Testament Isaac was born to Abraham, and Jacob was born to Isaac, and so on. John 3:6 makes plain, "That which is born of the flesh is flesh." Human beings are "intricately wrought" and we can marvel with the psalmist that we are "fearfully and wonderfully made" (Psalm 139:14).

But, born of the flesh as human beings to live on earth, we also should be born of the Spirit to become spiritual beings prepared for Heaven (John 3:5). When we behold the glory of Jesus, the only begotten of the Father, and willfully receive Him into our hearts, we become the children of God—new creations, spiritual beings! Because I was fascinated by the concept, I read John 3 over and over. One evening in 1970 I sat in my room at a women's retreat wondering what I was doing there. There was some time before the program started, so I started leafing through a magazine that had been left conveniently on my bed. A cartoon of a caterpillar caught my eye, and I began reading an article about what it meant to be born again.

With vague thoughts of the caterpillar, cocoon and butterfly floating in my mind, I rushed into the meeting a bit late. Sitting on the back row was fine with me, as it gave me a chance to look over these 200 strange women who carried Bibles and thought retreats were the greatest. They smiled, nodded, and took profuse notes—always laughing in unison, as if on cue.

The speaker who was from California spoke just like my Christian friends from Indianapolis! They all seemed to understand her, but I felt like a child with my nose pressed to the window of a candy store—on the outside, looking in! Especially, when she called attention to a piece of jewelry pinned to the tip of her shoulder. She explained how the beautiful, jeweled butterfly represented what had once been an ugly, hairy worm—scurrying in the dust, doing the best it could. But then it wove about itself a cocoon, choosing to die to its old way of life, and later it miraculously emerged a new creation—a butterfly. The scientists couldn't explain it, she said, but they called it metamorphosis.

"In the same way," she went on, "human beings scurry along in the dust of life doing the best they can. But when they hear the gospel they may choose to die to their old way of life by acknowledging sin, accepting forgiveness and His new life. When they do, they miraculously emerge spiritual beings. We can't explain this either," she assured us, "but Jesus called it being *born again.*" This phrase was not so widely used then as it is now.

It has always blessed me that the heavenly Father repeats things for slow learners. Now it was beginning to make sense! After a brief talk with the speaker, Vonette Bright, she led me in a prayer that I had prayed feverishly many times for six weeks. Only this time I was supernaturally born again!

What was it that had made the difference? Had I not said many prayers telling Jesus I heard His voice and was opening the door of my heart to receive Him into my life? Yes, I had done that. But *this* time I believed that not only was I willing to "do business with Him," but He was willing to "do business with me." Whether I felt or saw any visible evidence of His presence in my life no longer mattered. I quit calling God a liar and began taking Him at His word. I believed Him when He said, "Behold, I stand at the door and knock; if anyone hears My voice and opens the door, I will come in to him, and will dine with him, and he with Me" (Revelation 3:20). I claimed His promise: "If any man is in Christ, he is a new creature; the old things passed away; behold, new things have come" (2 Corinthians 5:17). I acknowledged with Paul, "and you were dead in your trespasses and sins" (Ephesians 2:1), but then I was made alive!

He gave me new life with the word of truth! I left the room in a quiet, contemplative mood. I was now a spiritual being, a child of God, a new creation. I had been born from above—a butterfly!

After the born-again experience, we begin to pursue spiritual maturity. As we do so, we should remember that we are not only human beings but spiritual beings. The standard of spiritual behavior in God's Word is impossible for mere human nature to live up to. We often forget that when we became spiritually reborn, we received a new nature, the nature of God, which empowers us to live according to His Word. Our human nature continues to dominate our lives. We are poor listeners. We talk too much, often regretting what we've said. Quick tempered and impatient, we open our mouth and insert our foot!

When we live in our human nature, relationships suffer, communications break down, and misunderstandings occur. James clearly perceived our humanness as he cautioned:

> This you know, my beloved brethren. But let everyone be quick to hear, slow to speak and slow to anger; for the anger of man does not achieve the righteousness of God. Therefore putting aside all filthiness and all that remains of wickedness, in humility receive the word implanted, which is able to save your souls (James 1:19-21).

The filthiness and wickedness in this verse probably refers to James' thoughts on lust and sin in verses 14 and 15. We are instructed to do the direct opposite of "what comes naturally."

The Word says that we can:

1. be a good listener—
"The ear of the wise seeks knowledge" (Proverbs 18:15);

2. be slow to speak—
"He who gives an answer before he hears,
It is folly and shame to him" (Proverbs 18:13),
"When there are many words, trangression is unavoidable,
But he who restrains his lips is wise" (Proverbs 10:19),
"And to make it your ambition to lead a quiet life" (1 Thessalonians 4:11);

3. be slow to anger—
"He who is slow to anger is better than the mighty,
And he who rules his spirit, than he who captures a city" (Proverbs 16:32);

4. put away all filthiness—
"If we say that we have not sinned, we make Him a liar, and His word is not in us" (1 John 1:10),
"No temptation has overtaken you but such as is common to man; and God is faithful, who will not allow you to be tempted beyond what you are able, but with the temptation will provide the way of escape also, that you may be able to endure it" (1 Corinthians 10:13).

In the first part of James, God challenges us to pursue spiritual maturity by rejoicing and considering it all joy. In the final two verses of the letter He challenges us to rebuke and exhort one another to turn from error. The goal is always holiness and requires more than human nature to attain. The path to spiritual maturity can only be walked in His power.

God said, "Be Holy, for I am Holy" (1 Peter 1:16) and He describes what that will mean in the life of His child. It will require "weeding and seeding" — putting away imbedded habits and sowing the seed of His Word into fertile, teachable hearts. His Word will enable us to be saved — day by day, moment by moment — from the power of sin, if we'll only take it seriously and apply it. Our homes would hum with happiness if we were consistently good listeners, choosing our words with careful thought, with our tempers in check. If His righteousness were overflowing in our hears, it would permeate our homes also. But only the Holy Spirit can enable us to be His holy children.

Our souls are saved from all they would do naturally by the Holy Spirit. The joy of pursuing maturity will depend upon our understanding of this holy person who has made our body His abode. Here are some basic truths concerning His vital role in our lives:

First, *every true believer is born again of the Spirit of God — the Holy Spirit.* He is the third person of the Trinity: God, the Father; God, the Son; and God, the Holy Spirit. God, the Holy Spirit, is a person. He has personality and is co-equal with the Father and the Son.

Perhaps you grew up in a church where you whispered His name because you didn't understand Him. Scripture says that our Christian life is going to depend on what we understand about Him!

As John 3:6 explains, "That which is born of the flesh is flesh." We entered this earth by physical birth. But when we receive Christ, we are born again of God's Holy Spirit. "That which is born of the Spirit is spirit." If He is in our lives, we would be wise to understand His mission.

Second, *every true believer is indwelt by the Holy Spirit of God.* In 1 Corinthians 6:19-20 we read:

> Or do you not know that your body is a temple of the Holy Spirit who is in you, whom you have from God, and that you are not your own? For you have been bought with a price: therefore glorify God in you body.

Many people say, "I've been a Christian always or for a long time, but I just received the Holy Spirit last year." Not according to Romans 8:9.

> However, you are not in the flesh but in the Spirit, if indeed the Spirit of God dwells in you. But if anyone does not have the Spirit of Christ, he does not belong to Him.

This clearly states that, if you are not indwelt by God's Spirit, you are *not* a Christian. Christian means "Christ in one," in the form of the Spirit. You don't receive the Spirit at some point after you become a Christian. When you receive Jesus, "in Him you have been made complete" (Colossians 2:10).

Third, *true believers are all baptized by the Holy Spirit*. This is another important point we mustn't miss. Since we are complete in Christ, we have received all that we're ever going to get. If we have not the Spirit, we are none of His. So this baptism of the Holy Spirit that is described in 1 Corinthians took place when we received Christ:

> For even as the body is one and yet has many members, and all the members of the body, though they are many, are one body, so also is Christ. For by one Spirit we were all baptized into one body, whether Jews or Greeks, whether slaves or free, and we were all made to drink of one Spirit. For the body is not one member, but many (1 Corinthians 12:12-14).

The Body of Christ is composed of those who have received Christ. The word "baptism" means "to plunge," or "to dip in." The purpose of the baptism in the Holy Spirit is to change and unite us with the body of Christ. We become one when we are dipped into Christ. Like dipping a piece of cloth into a dye, a lovely change takes place!

Fourth, *all true believers are sealed by the Holy Spirit of promise*. In Ephesians 1:13, 14 we are told that we have this seal upon us. We are marked people until the day we go to be with Jesus.

> In Him, you also, after listening to the message of truth, the gospel of your salvation — having also believed, you were sealed in Him with the Holy Spirit of promise, who is given as a pledge of our inheritance, with a view to the redemption of God's own possession, to the praise of His glory.

The Holy Spirit is like the down payment we place on a piece of real estate we intend to purchase. By this seal, God boldly declares us to be His property. He certainly paid a high enough price to purchase us from sin's destiny!

Fifth, *believers need to be filled with the Holy Spirit.* Four things have been given that are true of every person who has saving faith in Jesus: Born of, indwelt by, baptized in and sealed with the Holy Spirit. When we pause to contemplate the implications of this fact, it staggers us. But sometimes these statements roll glibly off our lips instead of putting us in awe of all the Lord God has done to save us and secure us for Himself!

In this fifth point we see that our will is involved. We must choose to be filled. One reason is to experience His power to live the Christian life. But more important than that is the fact that God commanded it!

> And do not get drunk with wine, for that is dissipation, but be filled with the Spirit (Ephesians 5:18).

Not to be filled with the Holy Spirit is to insist on being filled with self and to willfully deny His Lordship.

Someone once explained to me that God's Holy Spirit could not live through my life *before* I received Christ. That was the turning point for me, because it made sense. I had already tried hard to "play church" for thirty years, and it had never produced anything. The idea of committing myself to Christ, and then having to spend the next thirty years trying even harder to be a better Christian, sounded exhausting and impossible. Not because my outward life was so rotten, but because I knew my own heart and figured that it wasn't worth the struggle. It was hard enough *without* being truly committed to pleasing Jesus. I was afraid that if I made that commitment, it might not work. If you try God and *He* fails, where do you turn?

Then I was made to understand that when I did receive Christ, I would be born of His Spirit. If I would trust Him, He would enable me supernaturally to live the Christian life, which I was not capable of doing on my own.

After accepting Christ, it becomes clear that the Christian life is not hard—it is impossible! There's not one of us who can take the teachings of the Bible and consistently live by its high standards unless we have the Holy Spirit empowering us. The *same* resurrection power that raised Jesus from the dead is promised to make it possible to pursue spiritual maturity! That should bring joy to our ears. And yet, my heart grieves over people I see choosing to live in powerless, spiritual defeat.

The teaching on the Holy Spirit that I received before I accepted Christ, was in a booklet called, "Have You Made the Wonderful Discovery of the Spirit-filled Life?" It has been reproduced for you to read on pages 165-172.

This booklet helps us recognize the subtle sins of fear, worry and self-control. It is good to discover Scriptures that assure us of God's cleansing, peace and power. In spite of this, many *who know the contents of this booklet still live powerless lives.* There are many reasons for that, but *three* have come to my attention.

First, most people sincerely desire to be empowered by the Holy Spirit. It sounds marvelous to be able to draw on all the power we'll need to live an abundant life. The snag is the phrase "to be controlled by." Many want the power to *use* it like gasoline, but plan to continue charting their course themselves! How subtle it is to want power to do what *we* want to do. We might even have an endless list of good things we want to do for God. But we must allow *Him* to direct and control our lives *His* way. When we do, we acknowledge that He is Lord!

He insists on charting the course if He's going to provide the fuel. He has a course planned for each of us. It is perfect. But if He is not at the controls, we will certainly be detoured. In order to gain maturity, Christians must relinquish the controls to the one who knows the directions! We may want to be empowered, but are we willing to be directed?

The second reason people live powerless lives lies in the area of confessing sins. On page 172 you will find the concept of spiritual breathing as explained in the Holy Spirit booklet. We can exhale the impure by confession and inhale the pure by asking in faith to be filled with the Holy Spirit. The breakdown comes when we have diligently practiced this for many weeks or months, until it has become routine. Then we carelessly forget to practice. After all, we don't want to become *mechanical.* However, we cannot become neglectful either. The promise of 1 John 1:9 is *if* we confess our sins, He will forgive and cleanse. Another promise, in 1 John 5:14, 15 says that *if* we ask anything according to His will, He will hear us. And James 4:2 assures us that we do not have because we do not ask. He further reminds us that we often ask with wrong motives, and that leads to the denial of our request.

Perhaps seasoned Christians take forgiveness, cleansing and filling for granted. Can we remember the last time we consciously confessed a sin and *asked* to be filled with the Holy Spirit? Have we become so insensitive to sin that we fail to recognize it? When our hearts deceive us into thinking we're doing okay, we must allow *Him* to do the convicting! We must lament with the psalmist:

> Search me, O God, and know my heart; Try me, and know my anxious thoughts;
> And see if there be any hurtful way in me,
> And lead me in the everlasting way (Psalm 139:23, 24).

New Christians seeking maturity may try "spiritual breathing" for a while and become exasperated and exhausted. It seems more like "spiritual-gasping" to have to continually confess sins to remain in His light and power. At first, that's how it seemed to me. Gradually, I came to understand why.

In Luke 2 there is a simple phrase describing the birth of Jesus that sheds some light on our dilemma with "spiritual gasping." Verse 7 begins, "And she gave birth to her first-born son; and she wrapped him in cloths..." This verse depicts coming into this world physically. When I was born, I was "wrapped" with a culture, philosophy, and environment that contributed to my habits, ideas and activities.

Then I met Jesus, and was born again. It was like Lazarus being called forth from the grave. God made me, who had been dead in trespasses and sin, alive. But when Lazarus hobbled forth he discovered that he was bound head to toe in grave clothes. So was I. Although sincere in my desire to follow Jesus, there was a constant tripping over old habits, ideas, words and actions. I found I had 30 years of wrappings to contend with! Exhaling the impure and inhaling the pure seemed to be an ongoing, unending procedure. But I was encouraged with this thought: As we persist in seeking forgiveness, cleansing and filling from the Lord, we don't become sinless, but we do sin less and less.

Losing my temper, for example, was a constant problem. Anger seemed to erupt dozens of times each day. Life was so exasperating! Several months later, after one thousand exhales and inhales, there did come a time when I could see a measurable difference in how often anger got the best of me. And now, after ten years, it is no longer a besetting sin — only an occasional visitor that has to be dealt with.

No matter how long we have known Christ, we must keep practicing! If we ask the Lord to help us see sin the way He does, we may be filled as often as we detect anything contrary to the fruit of the Spirit. We cannot rationalize and make excuses! Jesus didn't die for our excuses — neither does He condone them!

The third reason for spiritual power failure is that we do not present every area of our lives to God. Romans 12:1 states that we are to present our bodies "a living and holy sacrifice, acceptable to God." Yet, Christians section off their lives like slices of a pie — reserving certain pieces for their own control.

We are like the new wineskins Jesus spoke of in Luke 5. We have a new heart (new wineskin) that is softened to the things of God (new wine) and yet "no one, after drinking old wine [old life, old pleasures, old habits] wishes for new; for he says, 'The old is good enough'" (Luke 5:39). We are grateful for salvation and growth in His Word. But there are a few areas where we would just rather the Lord would leave us alone.

Perhaps it is only *one* resentment that we would like to harbor or one habit we would like to enjoy. But no matter how we rationalize, explain and put off dealing with that *one* area, as long as we try to mix old wine with new, we are nothing short of "mixed bags!" And God will not supernaturally empower a mixed bag. We don't have to be perfect before God will fill us. But we must be living in the light He has given us and present every area to His gracious control.

As you consider whether you have honestly presented *every* area of your body to God as a living sacrifice, remember Ananias and Sapphira . They professed to have given all when they hadn't. The Holy Spirit removed them from the scene. God hates sham and will *not* impart His power to a life that pretends. This is why James stressed in Chapter 1, verses 18-21:

> In the exercise of His will He brought us forth by the word of truth, so that we might be, as it were, the first fruits among His creatures.
>
> This you know, my beloved brethren. But let everyone be quick to hear, slow to speak and slow to anger; for the anger of man does not achieve the righteousness of God.
>
> Therefore putting aside all filthiness and all that remains of wickedness, in humility receive the word implanted, which is able to save your souls.

We *can* be good listeners, sensitive conversationalists, with controlled tempers. If we will put away all filthiness and overflowing of wickedness, we can receive God's Word and remain sensitive to the conditions He has given for knowing His fullness.

We are begotten by a Father who desires to wrap us in His swaddling clothes. He wishes to fill our new wineskins (hearts) with His wine and save our souls eternally from the old wine — our old ways. This work of God is sanctification, the path to maturity. And He has allowed us to choose our course. We can be powerless, spiritual casualties who refuse to yield every area to His cleansing and control, or we can respond to His power.

Reflect and Act

Which of these reasons for continuing in powerless defeat most often describes you?
— lacking the *sincere desire* to be DIRECTED by God,
— consistently acknowledging and confessing sin, with the intention to forsake it,
— failing to present EVERY area of life to God.

From day to day, which area gives you the most difficulty?
— too talkative,
— easily discouraged,
— quick tempered.

Write a prayer to the Lord about these areas of weakness, claiming His cleansing, filling and victory. (Determine to persist in seeking cleansing and filling in these areas *repeatedly* until you see *consistent* victory.)

Chapter 8

Walking In The
Perfect Law of Liberty
James 1:22-25

22 But prove yourselves doers of the word, and not
merely hearers who delude themselves. 23 For if anyone is
a hearer of the word and not a doer, he is like a man who
looks at his natural face in a mirror: 24 for *once* he has
looked at himself and gone away, he has immediately forgot-
ten what kind of person he was. 25 But one who looks intently at the perfect law, the *law* of liberty, and abides by
it, not having become a forgetful hearer but an effectual
doer, this man shall be blessed in what he does.

A WOMAN stands in front of a mirror and takes inventory. Her
hair is a mess. It is straight, stringy and disheveled. Her eyebrows
need tweezing, and there's a smudge on her cheek. Her mascara
has smeared, giving her two black eyes. Colorless and gray, she
needs lipstick and rouge. She definitely needs some attention!
The mirror has delivered its message — loud and clear!

However, this woman simply walks away from the mirror
to begin the day's activities, immediately forgetting what she has
seen. Is this act believable? Unless she's competing for the "Alice
Goon-Girl" award, instinct would drive her to do more than walk
away from such a clear warning. Any woman would be a fool
to think that she could continue through the day in that condition, and go unnoticed.

It is one thing to read through the Book of James. It is
another thing to live it! God's Word was never meant only to

stimulate our imaginations or intellects. It was meant to be believed and acted upon. Yet many come and go from church or Bible studies appearing like the disheveled woman who walks away from a mirror ignoring its warning. By asking several questions, we discover that James in these verses presents some reasons we don't see the Word of God changing more lives.

1. *Have we been liberated by becoming enslaved to the Word?* We will not be "diligent doers" of the Word until we have discovered that it is the perfect law of liberty that *blesses* the doer.

Satan has convinced Christians that to live by God's Word is to be in a straight jacket — boxed-in misery. Quite the opposite is true. To be enslaved to God's Word is to be liberated! It is the law of life! Jesus, the Word made flesh, came to give us abundant life! Knowing this, Satan has convinced the world that God wants to make us miserable with a long list of do's and don'ts. There is a fine line between this legalistic list, which encourages hypocrisy, and obedience to God's commands, which sets us free to bless ourselves and God. The division is between those who cherish and serve "a system" and those who love and obey their Father, the one who left them a love letter and the power to obey it. A love letter is not something to be glanced over and filed away on a shelf to gather dust. It is to be pored over, cherished, and responded to *in love*. We cannot be liberated by it, if we don't see it leading us in love.

2. *Have we asked God to give us "spiritual discernment"?* One of the most troubling things we face in Bible-teaching churches and Bible studies today is a noticeable lack of discernment on the part of believers. There is often a real insensitivity to right and wrong, good and evil. Christians often discuss a situation in light of "the times we are living in" and this becomes an *excuse* for their unbiblical behavior. They condone, rationalize or neglect to view the circumstance according to the Word. In doing so, they deceive themselves.

One Sunday recently, I watched several practicing adulterers enter church, sit down, and listen to the message. They departed with no apparent intentions of being doers of the Word. Has the twentieth century produced a new brand of believers swayed by the world, the flesh and the devil, who hear God's Word, but who do not bother to act on it? No. The apathy of the times is not totally responsible. The problems have long existed. Ezekiel noticed them.

"And they come to you as people come, and sit before you as My people, and hear your words, but they do not do them, for they do the lustful desires expressed by their mouth, and their heart goes after their gain" (Ezekiel 33:31).

Those words could easily have been written by a twentieth century pastor who is watching his flock choose not to *do* what the Word has said!

We can't pray for discernment if we aren't doers of the Word. We can't pray for liberated spirits or blessing if we don't follow the commandments. There is a great deal to be gained if we truly value discernment, liberty and blessing from God. His Word is not a collection of platitudes that we can occasionally read and then disregard! We deceive ourselves if we think we can play church or run from study to study and not face accountability. Hebrews 4:12 cautions that we are playing with danger when we handle God's Word! It's like a two-edged sword, quick and powerful which discerns the thoughts and intentions of our hearts!

3. *Have we made the choice to "grow up"?* The Word is both milk and solid food. It is quite clear in 1 Peter 2:2 that baby Christians need to start with "milk." They need to understand their salvation, the gospel, and the work of the cross. Babies need milk.

But mature Christians will hear the meat of the Word and do it. God does not want His children to fail to mature any more than we would choose to have a retarded child or slow learner. I pity the pastor who needs to change, powder and diaper half of his congregation each week. He has to give them a bottle, because they fail to be doers of the Word, walking in obedience. They *come, sit* and *hear,* but they won't do. They take in, but they won't put out. These words from Hebrews say it well:

> Concerning him we have much to say, and it is hard to explain, since you have become dull of hearing. For though by this time you ought to be teachers, you have need again for someone to teach you the elementary principles of the oracles of God, and you have come to need milk and not solid food. For everyone who partakes only of milk is not accustomed to the word of righteousness, for he is a babe. But solid food is for the mature, who because of practice have their senses trained to discern good and evil. (Hebrews 5:11-14).

If Christians cannot distinguish good from evil, we might just as well color our world gray and shout "anything goes!"

But God does not want us to live in a dull, lawless world. As James points out, He wants us to "look into the perfect law of liberty" and do what His Word instructs. Then we can be discerning and helpful to those who are lost in a fuzzy maze of "no absolutes," situation ethics and amorality.

Our choice is whether we are going to be discerning or deceived. If we choose to be children, we'll be deceived. If we decide to "grow up," God will give us discernment. The church was designed to contain Christians who have chosen to be doers of the Word and will assume responsibility to support others in the faith.

> As a result, we are no longer to be children, tossed here and there by waves, and carried about by every wind of doctrine, by the trickery of men, by craftiness in deceitful scheming; but speaking the truth in love, we are to grow up in all aspects into Him, who is the head, even Christ (Ephesians 4:14, 15).

As this passage in Ephesians shows, God doesn't intend for us to remain children. It is God's plan that the church mature by "speaking the truth in love."

4. *Have we begun to be a doer of the Word and then failed to continue?* We often begin a project with the best intentions and then get side-tracked. Our problem is that we're forgetful. A form of the word forget is used twice in verses 24 and 25 of James chapter 1, but the principle is repeated throughout Scripture. In the Old and New Testaments, the prophets and apostles reminded the people of what they needed to know and do, because they were forgetful too. The following verses illustrate the importance of being reminded constantly:

> Remind them of these things . . . (2 Timothy 2:14).
> "And you shall remember all the way which the Lord your God has led you in the wilderness these forty years . . ." (Deuteronomy 8:2).
> Remember His wonders which He has done . . . (Psalm 105:5).
> "Remember the former things long past,
> For I am God, and there is no other . . ." (Isaiah 46:9).
> "In everything I showed you that by working hard in this manner you must help the weak and remember the words of the Lord Jesus, that He Himself said, 'It is more blessed to give than to receive'" (Acts 20:35).

Therefore, I shall always be ready to remind you of these things, even though you already know them, and have been established in the truth which is present with you. And I consider it right, as long as I am in this earthly dwelling, to stir you up by way of reminder (2 Peter 1:12, 13).

Unfortunately, we don't begin a pattern of consistent doing by hearing something only once. We're just not wired that way! Because we are "forgetful hearers", we need to be reminded again and again. Therefore we must be sitting under the Word's influence constantly. The goal of teaching and ministering is not to come up with something clever and new — but to remind Christians of what they already know. Why is this necessary? So that they'll "continue in it," rather than "forget."

What is it that we so easily forget? We need constant reminding of the basics. Not deeper truths — but the basics. While it is beneficial to attend a prophecy conference or study some Bible truth in great depth, when the stresses of daily life hit, we need the basics. We cannot let our minds be corrupted from "the simplicity that is in Christ."

Use this checklist to remind yourself of what the Word requires:

— Am I giving thanks in all things?
— Am I turning my cheek when someone offends me?
— Have I forgiven? Is there any root of bitterness strangling me?
— Am I calling sin *Sin*?
— Have I confessed and forsaken that sin?
— Am I witnessing? Praying? Practicing and remembering to do what His Word has instructed? Am I consistently exposed to teaching which reminds me to continue in the Word?

Our answers to these questions may determine our future Christian growth.

5. *Have we set a goal to be a success or a failure?* Absurd, you say? Not really. There was a time in my life when I was destined to be a "successful failure." When my husband and I were new Christians, we attended a series of lectures given by Dr. Bob Smith. He related a story that has helped mold my attitude about being a doer of the Word. Perhaps this paraphrase of the story will explain what I mean by successful failure:

There was a man who sought the advice of a godly counselor because his life was suddenly in shambles. He sat broken, sobbing repeatedly, "I'm a failure! I'm a failure!" The listener encouraged him to calm down and explain what he meant.

Sadly, his tale spilled out. "As a young man I determined to have all the things I had been deprived of as a child. When I married, I promised my wife a beautiful home, opportunities to travel and see the world, a closet full of beautiful clothes and the best education for our children. I also determined to provide my mother with a comfortable home and other pleasures she had never enjoyed.

"I've worked hard and achieved every one of those goals! And then, just this week, my wife told me she is leaving me. She complained that she is tired of raising the children alone. None of these things I provided made her happy. I'm a failure! I'm a miserable failure!" the man lamented, and his voice became lost in deep sobs.

The counselor listened to all that he had to say. He realized that this Christian man and his family had been attending a Bible teaching church for years. He had never intentionally set the goal of becoming a failure, and yet that was how he now saw himself.

"You're not a failure," the counselor replied. "You're a success. You have achieved every goal that you set for yourself. But you are a 'successful failure,' because you set the wrong goals."

This story is a sober warning to stop and look where we're heading. "There is a way which seems right to a man, but its end is the way of death" (Proverbs 16:25). Have we chosen God's path of joy or the road to sad success? Joy is always discovered in the "perfect law of liberty." That is why Joshua was instructed to meditate on it day and night:

> "This book of the law shall not depart from your mouth, but you shall meditate on it day and night, so thay so you may be careful to do according to all that is written in it; for then you will make your way prosperous, and then you will have success" (Joshua 1:8).

According to the goals we establish, we can become either a successful failure or a sincere success.

6. *Would we rather be a "squash" or a "mighty oak"?* When I first started attending Bible study, I was challenged constantly to take God and His Word seriously and not to settle for "instant cures," "instant pleasure" or "instant success." Life just isn't like that because growing up takes time. One of the ways our teacher

impressed this upon me was through the simple question I raised above—"Would you rather be a 'squash' or a 'Mighty Oak'?"

When she further explained that God could make a squash in six months, but it took years for Him to make a mighty oak, I began to see the point. We live in an "instant" society, but that does not alter physical and spiritual laws. It takes time to grow mighty and strong.

With that simple illustration in mind, I decided to be a mighty oak. If I had the choice of the kind of soil my heart could be, I wanted to be good ground—able to bear much fruit. God gives us that choice. He revealed in Psalm 1:1-3 that the man who continues in His Word will be blessed:

> How blessed is the man who does not walk in the counsel
> of the wicked,
> Nor stand in the path of sinners,
> Nor sit in the seat of scoffers!
> But his delight is in the law of the Lord,
> And in His law he meditates day and night.
> And he will be like a tree firmly planted by streams of water,
> Which yields its fruit in its season,
> And its leaf does not wither;
> And in whatever he does, he prospers.

There are some requirements, however, when we choose to be mighty oaks. It requires patiently *continuing* in the Word day and night. The fruit is not "instant" but comes forth "in its season"—in God's timing. Mighty oaks are seldom seen in the midst of a forest surrounded by clusters of tall, spindly, barren trees. They are usually found standing alone . . . weathered and strengthened by winds and storms that hit their unprotected frame.

Often what we think is our protected forest—a holy huddle of believers—turns out instead to be a parched place. When we try to lean on one another to survive the storms, we dry up like a desert shrub. But Jeremiah describes prosperity for the man who trusts God when the storms come. This man is blessed:

> Thus says the Lord,
> "Cursed is the man who trusts in mankind
> And makes flesh his strength,
> And whose heart turns away from the Lord.
> For he will be like a bush in the desert
> And will not see when prosperity comes,

But will live in stony wastes in the wilderness,
A land of salt without inhabitant.
Blessed is the man who trusts in the Lord
And whose trust is the Lord.
For he will be like a tree planted by the water,
That extends its roots by a stream
And will not fear when the heat comes;
But its leaves will be green,
And it will not be anxious in a year of drought
Nor cease to yield fruit" (Jeremiah 17:5-8).

We have to be planted in the Word, with our roots going deep . . . because the "droughts" will come.

After deciding to be a mighty oak, I began to become an obedient woman of the Word, a doer as well as a hearer. It seemed to be the only sane thing to do because Jesus warned of the consequences of *not* doing it in Luke, chapter 6.

"And why do you call Me, 'Lord, Lord,' and do not do what I say? Everyone who comes to Me, and hears My words, and acts upon them, I will show you whom he is like: he is like a man building a house, who dug deep and laid a foundation upon the rock; and when a flood rose, the torrent burst against that house and could not shake it, because it had been well built. But the one who has heard, and has not acted accordingly, is like a man who built a house upon the ground without any foundation; and the torrent burst against it and immediately it collapsed, and the ruin of that house was great" (Luke 6:46-49).

Whether the comparison is to a mighty oak or a solid house, the message is the same. Will we live our life our way or God's way? Our choice is to be either discerning or deceived. We can walk as babes or mature Christians, as forgetful hearers or continuous rememberers. Our decision will determine if we become successful failures or sincere successes. Our growth will be quick like a feeble squash or enduring as the strong oak. The house will be built on a solid foundation which stands or on a weak base that brings destruction. As we become a doer of the Word, our faith will be tested, purified, strengthened and proven!

Strangely enough, fried egg sandwiches with mayonnaise and tomato soup with butter floating on the top has become a symbol to me, and others, of a life stabilized in the storm. I had known the Lord less than two months when I asked Him to work in me "both to will and to work for His good pleasure" (Philippians 2:13). And now I sat in our living room, wondering if my husband would ever come home. This was obviously another "night on the town" because he had not arrived or called at dinner time. It was apparent that our marriage was in serious trouble. How desperately my Dave needed a Savior, so that we could begin to sweep away the decay and build our home upon the Rock!

I watched the clock until two, then three in the morning. As I waited, God showed me Scriptures that declare His sovereign control—His power to work on our behalf. I knew that when Dave walked through the front door, I would be faced with a choice. I could react my way, even though the yelling and crying had failed previously to bring about the change I sought. Or I could choose God's way and be slow to speak, slow to anger, and forgiving.

When three-thirty arrived, the door slowly opened and the poor man literally fell through. As he did so, he caught his thumb on the door knob, jamming it. There he lay, a pitiful specimen of manhood. He raised up, smiled and said, "I'm hungry!"

Since he was on the floor, it would be easy to kick him and tell him that was *his* problem. And don't think the idea wasn't tempting! *Or* I could quietly give thanks in all things—consider it joy, and trust that God would use this opportunity to work it for good. It wouldn't hurt, I reasoned, to take God at His Word and see how He could "bless this mess!" My problems weren't too big for God! I had only been a Christian a few weeks, and it was time to "dabble at doing" to discover His "perfect law of liberty!"

Helping Dave to his feet, I took him to the breakfast room table and proceeded to fix his favorite—his *very* favorite meal, fried egg sandwiches with mayonnaise, and tomato soup with butter floating on top. He stared in amazement for a few minutes. Then I saw the familiar vein begin to rise on his forehead as he turned red, pounded his fists on the table and yelled, "Why don't you get mad?"

Inside I silently took control over my reaction. *Be slow to speak, girl. Don't blow it now! Don't preach and don't explode; just tell him why.* The answer came simply out of a heart that was filled with love and concern for this frustrated husband. "Because, honey, I've been doing that for ten years and it hasn't gotten us anyplace."

That early morning, his soup and sandwiches were served in the might and powerful love of Christ. I was just beginning to see, as James predicted, the blessing reserved for those who will look intently at the perfect law of liberty and abide by it, not having become a forgetful hearer but an effectual *doer*.

Today this same man is the spiritual leader in our home. He teaches the Bible to several hundred business and professional men who have spent a good part of their lives being "successful failures." Dave's salvation one month after that incident also saved our marriage and our home. The storms have still come, and the droughts have hit. That's life! But now we're constantly *reminding* each other of the need to *continue* to sink our roots deep — to be constant in the Word, *hear* it and *do* it.

Soon after we moved to Philadelphia, I received an opportunity to teach these scriptural concepts to a group of 150 women. I was relating experiences and challenging those women to be mighty oaks for God. I assured them it wouldn't happen overnight and that the storms might be painful. Following the message, a beautiful woman, who had a big tear about to drop onto her cheek, approached me. "Dianne," she said timidly, "I'd like to be a mighty oak."

I soon learned that Patsy had just accepted Christ after many years in psychiatric therapy trying to overcome "agraphobia," a condition of being paralyzed by fears. She had not driven for 15 years, could not be alone in her house, walk to the mailbox alone or handle train rides or tunnels. The first verses of Scripture to grip Patsy's heart once she received Christ, began to transform her life. Jesus said, "If you abide in My word, then you are truly disciples of Mine; and you shall know the truth, and the truth shall make you *free*" (John 8:31, 32).

That's all the encouragement Patsy needed to "look into the perfect law of liberty" and continue in it. The results have been miraculous. Today, she drives, loves being alone, travels on trains and through tunnels. For her, "His power is perfected in weakness" (2 Corinthians 12:9). Only five years have passed, but she's in the process of becoming a mighty oak.

While it is true that we live fragmented lives, fulfilling many roles and meeting numerous needs, we *can* be fruitful for God in the process rather than frazzled failures, We *do* have a choice. Each of us has a throne in our hearts. Colossians 3:15 encourages us to "let the peace of Christ rule in your hearts, to which indeed you were called in one body; and be thankful." As James teaches, the Prince of Peace will rule only in a heart yielded to God's "game plan"—the perfect law of liberty. The man who chooses this path of joy will constantly abide in His Word and perform it. When he does so, he will be certain to reap supernatural blessings.

Reflect and Act

Take a look in the mirror. Do you see a person who is:
liberated because of being *enslaved* to the Word of God?
spiritually discerning?
"growing up" spiritually?
forgetting or remembering to live up to what you know?
setting goals and moving toward them?
satisfied to be a "squash" or pressing on to be a "mighty oak"?

Now, complete this statement:
If I were to take what God has said (in James 1:22-23) about being a DOER of the Word SERIOUSLY...I would have to

PART II

God's Fine Tuning

Chapter 9

Partiality Poisons Joy
James 1:26—2:13

26 If anyone thinks himself to be religious, and yet does not bridle his tongue but deceives his *own* heart, this man's religion is worthless. 27 This is pure and undefiled religion in the sight of *our* God and Father, to visit orphans and widows in their distress, *and* to keep oneself unstained by the world.

The Sin of Partiality

2 MY brethren, do not hold your faith in our glorious Lord Jesus Christ with *an attitude of* personal favoritism. 2 For if a man comes into your assembly with a gold ring and dressed in fine clothes, and there also comes in a poor man in dirty clothes, 3 and you pay special attention to the one who is wearing the fine clothes, and say, "You sit here in a good place," and you say to the poor man, "You stand over there, or sit down by my footstool." 4 have you not made distinctions among yourselves, and become judges with evil motives? 5 Listen, my beloved brethren: did not God choose the poor of this world *to be* rich in faith and heirs of the kingdom which He promised to those who love Him? 6 But you have dishonored the poor man. Is it not the rich who oppress you and personally drag you into court? 7 Do they not blaspheme the fair name by which you have been called? 8 If, however, you are fulfilling the royal law, according to the Scripture, "YOU SHALL LOVE YOUR NEIGHBOR AS YOURSELF," you are doing well. 9 But if you show partiality, you are committing sin *and* are convicted by the law as trangressors. 10 For whoever keeps the whole law and yet stumbles in one *point*, he has become guilty of

all. 11 For He who said, "Do not commit adultery," also said, "Do not commit murder." Now if you do not commit adultery, but do commit murder, you have become a trangressor of the law. 12 So speak and so act, as those who are to be judged by *the* law of liberty. 13 For judgment *will* be merciless to one who has shown no mercy: mercy triumphs over judgment.

HAVE YOU ever been guilty of being a "respecter of persons" in any of your church relationships? Have you ever been tempted to show partiality to some at the exclusion of others? Most of us would initially react to these questions with alarm. "God forbid that I would ever be guilty of such things." But if God did not feel it necessary to alert us to this problem, why did He reserve 13 verses of the second chapter of James to talk about partiality in the local church? Why did He paint a vivid picture of some being honored and others left out — right in the midst of a worship service? Could it be that He saw partiality infecting His beautiful church? Since the way we relate to each other is a reoccuring theme in the Bible, perhaps we need some fine tuning in this creeping, crippling matter of being a "respecter of persons."

Partiality poisons joy. It creates pride in the one being preferred, loneliness in the person being left out and poison in the individual being partial. Are we to treat each other in a way that thrills God's heart or grieves His Spirit? For example, there may be a woman in your church or neighborhood who has recently lost her husband. The first time you saw her after it happened, she revealed how lonely she is, not being included in mixed gatherings. You listened patiently, nodding your head as though you really understood. Inwardly you winced at the idea that you too might have to face the death of a loved one someday.

You thought of your busy schedule and wondered where you could carve out the time to "visit the fatherless and widows in their affliction."

Did your trite phrases or well-meaning thoughts really help? Was it easier to stay too busy to get involved?

You probably told her you love her and that the two of you must get together soon. You patted her hand, assured her of your continued prayers and explained something about the rush you were in as you scurried on breathlessly. You jotted a note to yourself to call or write next week. You meant well! You really did.

This scene could be multiplied by the number of widows we know. Add to that number the divorcees who are suffering a sense of loss and rejection, and the needs are overwhelming!

How often we mean well and babble on with our "good intentions." But people who are hurting need more than "high aims." If a person is "all smoke and no fire"—plenty of words, but no action—he is accused of possessing vain religion. Definitions for vain religion and pure religion are given in the last two verses of James, chapter 1:

> If anyone thinks himself to be religious, and yet does not bridle his tongue but deceives his own heart, this man's religion is worthless. This is pure and undefiled religion in the sight of our God and Father, to visit orphans and widows in their distress, and to keep oneself unstained by the world (James 1:26-27).

Vain religion is revealed through the unbridled tongue. The tongue is discussed in detail in chapter 3 but it applies to this issue too. In our talk with the widow, the unbridled tongue was simply rattling off a lot of good intentions that would never become actions, and that made all that was said vain and meaningless.

Pure religion is explicitly described as the act of visiting the fatherless and widows in their affliction and keeping oneself unspotted from the world. The combination of the two describes *sanctification.*

To visit the fatherless and the widows in their affliction doesn't mean to make a duty call and consider it done. That's legalistic and only serves to salve our conscience. James is speaking of taking an ongoing interest, and that is costly! It is true that our lives are busy. "But," the Lord nudges, "if your 'religion' is pure because you have a heart indwelt by the Holy Spirit and cleansed by the blood of Christ, you will *never* be too busy for needy, hurting people! When many are lonely, missing their daddy or their mate, God instructs us to care.

We are partial and "respecters of persons" if we cannot find the time to get involved with those who hurt. Our natural tendency is to gravitate toward happy people who are on the move— stimulating good times and happy memories. But pure religion is designed to be selfless and "others-centered." We hope experience has taught us there is no more lasting joy than to drop *everything* to respond to the need of another.

The personality, social status or reputation of the person is not to be considered. If the need is close enough to recognize, it is near enough to be satisfied. No one needs to qualify to receive our good deeds. Expressing love toward our neighbors, as good samaritans would, is what God is looking for. Pure religion springs from a pure heart, not a partial one!

It is sad to see scriptural examples of partiality among parents. These parents' acts of partiality resulted in irrevocable consequences and heartache. Isaac favored his elder son, Esau, while his wife, Rebecca, preferred their younger son, Jacob. As the problem intensified, Jacob actually had to flee for his life with the help of his mother. He did not return until after his mother's death. Partiality poisons joy.

Just as his mother and father had done, Jacob demonstrated partiality toward his eleventh son, Joseph, who was rejected by his brothers, cast into a pit, and sold into slavery. His being given a special present, the coat of many colors, resulted in his imprisonment and separation from home and country. Partiality poisons joy.

If partiality could be in the heart of a parent, it also could slip into our *conversation* (the unbridled tongue), our *works* (visiting the fatherless and widows) or our *worship*. When we come to church, it is to involve ourselves in worship to God! And yet, according to James, when we promenade and goggle at others, our conduct blasphemes the name *Christian*.

> My brethren, do not hold your faith in our glorious Lord Jesus Christ with an attitude of personal favoritism. For if a man comes into your assembly with a gold ring and dressed in fine clothes, and there also comes in a poor man in dirty clothes, and you pay special attention to the one who is wearing the fine clothes, and say, "You sit here in a good place," and you say to the poor man, "You stand over there, or sit down by my footstool," have you not made distinctions among yourselves, and become judges with evil motives? (James 2:1-4).

Faith in the Lord which allows acts of partiality is *inconsistent*. We can't profess faith in Christ on one hand and be partial on the other. If we do, we are letting ourselves become spotted by the world, rather than allowing Christ's blood to cleanse us. God wants to break us of "looking on the outward appearance," and fine tune us to "look on the heart." He realizes we are daz-

zled by jewels and designer labels and can easily slip into the ritual
of religion, losing sight of the *reality* of worship. This will happen, if we start focusing on one another, "jockeying for position" in God's Kingdom. Paul instructed the Corinthian church
that "there should be no division in the body, but that the members
should have *the same care* for one another" (1 Corinthians 12:25).

As the Lord patiently fine tunes us, the results are sometimes
humorous. He simply will not let us get away with "doing what
comes naturally" when He can do it *super*-naturally. A beautiful
example of this occurred in a city we once lived in.

The church in that city was affluent and naturally drew emi-
nent people. The congregation was being taught the Word of God
faithfully, and their desire was to follow Jesus. But their possessions opened the door to possible pride or a focus on prominence.

Suddenly, tragedy struck, and one of the families lost three
little children. The father of these children came from a distance
to attend the funeral. His background was different from his
wife's. He had lived a life with the circus, and he seemed to be
covered head to toe with tattoos! His hair was down to his
shoulders and bathing wasn't one of his favorite activities. His
clothes would have fit the King James description of "vile
raiment."

But God, who looks on the heart, used His Word to save
this man's soul at the funeral! The man was immediately
transformed. He decided to stay in town for a while and appeared
at that church with a Bible tucked under his arm. Not wanting
to be distracted by sitting in the back, he marched down the aisle
to the front pew. His heart was transformed, but his outward
appearance remained the same. God's dear "babe in Christ" per-
sonified an opportunity for all.

The godly woman who related this to me rejoiced over the
humbling the congregation endured as they greeted, accepted and
loved this man in the name of Christ. She admitted that it was
harder for some than for others, and I'm sure there were those
who never revealed that they were "respecters of persons" where
this brother was concerned.

The Word clearly warns us not to be judgmental. James 2:4
indicates that when we show favoritism, we have evil thoughts.
These evil thoughts might include how to keep the poor person
out of sight to save the respectable, affluent image of the congregation, how to explain his presence to visitors or what con-

tribution he could possibly make.

Similarly, evil surmisings could be directed to the one shown preference. After all, he is a rich man, in fine apparel. "If we treat him right, he would be a valuable asset because of his money and influence." How sinful for a church member to look into a man's pocket and potential for giving, rather than into his heart to see if it beats for God! Dare we let a church budget cause us to rely on man to meet needs rather than on the Lord? Partiality poisons joy and misplaces faith. James warns against this kind of prejudice:

> Listen, my beloved brethren: did not God choose the poor of this world to be rich in faith and heirs of the kingdom which He promised to those who love Him? But you have dishonored the poor man. Is it not the rich who oppress you and personally drag you into court? Do they not blaspheme the fair name by which you have been called? (James 2:5-7)

In this discussion of the rich, James accuses them of dishonoring, oppressing and persecuting the poor -- the very ones the Lord has chosen to bless with the riches of faith and His eternal inheritance. The rich who behave in such a way are said to blaspheme the name of Christians.

When our conduct does an injustice to the title of Christian, it dishonors the name of Christ Himself! The rich described in these verses are professing Christians. Our actions as the church body reflect on the one who is the Head of the church. If His Word is obeyed by loving our brother, we become a reflection of His love. As John put it:

> In this is love, not that we loved God, but that He loved us and sent His Son to be the propitiation for our sins. Beloved, if God so loved us, we also ought to love one another (1 John 4:10-11).

For some it is humbling to realize what a "motly crew" the Lord has called to Himself. We don't have to be in the body of Christ long to discover the truth of the camel getting through the eye of the needle being easier than the rich man laying aside all his possessions and confessing his need for Jesus. To receive Christ is not to be compared with joining a country club or any other exclusive group. "Whoever will may come" is God's invitation. When we think of the variety of people who have responded to this generous invitation, we realize heaven must be an interesting place!

But until we can be in the sinless environment of heaven, we are warned that we must identify and deal with partiality in our lives. Our joy in earth's "boot camp" depends on it!

Since our ministry in Philadelphia deals primarily with the business and professional community, we attempt to teach young Christians not to be exclusive in their worship and fellowship. Most of the men who attend my husband's Bible study belong to country clubs! Although we move in executive circles, we are also blessed by a few men who attend in overalls, attired for jobs that would muddy a white shirt and silk tie. God's love and Kingdom are not exclusive! Because these men are not respecters of persons, the group has grown to more than 250.

God seems to insist that the old adage, "a chain is only as strong as its weakest link," is true in spiritual life. Perhaps in some cases He is using a "motly crew" to bless His more distinguished children. Evaluate your own Bible study by the standards in James chapter 2:

> If, however, you are fulfilling the royal law, according to the Scripture, "You shall love your neighbor as yourself," you are doing well. But if you show partiality, you are committing sin and are convicted by the law as transgressors. For whoever keeps the whole law and yet stumbles in one point, he has become guilty of all. For He who said, "Do not commit adultery," also said, "Do not commit murder." Now if you do not commit adultery, but do commit murder, you have become a transgressor of the law. So speak and so act, as those who are to be judged by the law of liberty. For judgment will be merciless to one who has shown no mercy; mercy triumphs over judgment (James 2:8-13).

God will not allow sturdy links like loving our neighbor and avoiding murder and adultery to operate along with weak links such as partiality. If we indulge in any area that the Word calls sin, even if all else is of love, we have transgressed His law.

Jesus promised that as we come to know the truth, the truth will set us free! But we have to remember James' admonition to be doers of the Word and not hearers only. We simply delude ourselves when we fail to apply the truth to our lives. Peter emphasized what acting on the Word will accomplish:

> For such is the will of God that by doing right you may silence the ignorance of foolish men. Act as free men, and

do not use your freedom as a covering for evil, but use it as bondslaves of God (1 Peter 2:15-16).

God's truth liberates when it is obeyed. According to James 2:12, this perfect law of liberty will be the standard our lives are judged by. Our judgment will be without mercy if we have shown none to others. Fortunately, mercy will triumph over judgment.

We have seen how attitudes of preference toward others are devastating for the giver and the receiver. But what should be our response if *we* are being treated with partiality? I am not speaking of social etiquette or protocol that we must graciously submit to occasionally. Obviously, when I am a speaker at a large banquet, I do not insist on sitting in the back of the room. That would be false humility when people have gone to great lengths to create a smooth-running program and desire me to be near the microphone when it is time to speak. In reality, I am there to serve as I stand to share God's Word and my testimony.

But what of the times when someone, for no apparent reason, makes a fuss over you, leaving others to feel inferior or slighted? I found myself in such a situation last summer when I attended a lovely luncheon with a friend. The food had already been served when we arrived late and looked around for seats. Because my companion served on the board of this historic event, she was quickly asked to sit at the head table. And since I enjoy meeting new people, I prepared to slip into one of the few remaining seats in the back of the huge dining room.

My idea was quickly overruled. Someone knew that my associate was bringing a guest, so all of a sudden this lovely lady swished me through the room to a front row table. In essence she graciously was telling me, "Sit thou here in a good place" while others are still trying to find seats in the back. She was being quite loving to me, her "neighbor." But as I was seated, I had the distinct feeling it was going to be an uphill battle with the nine other ladies at my table. They had been told not to let anyone sit there, so they knew I had been given "preferred" treatment. And partiality poisons joy! I saw that several were not enthusiastic over my arrival. One honest soul even piped, "You must be someone *very* important to have a seat saved for you." They began to question who I was. It would have been easy to tell them the truth—no one special. But that would not have stirred their joy or satisfied their curiosity.

Wondering how to respond, I claimed James 1:5, asking for liberal wisdom. I eagerly accepted the challenge to allow God to "defuse" this situation. Although I had been forced on them when they had come so early to get their good seats, each of these women could leave the luncheon considering it all joy.

Conversation about Jesus and questions about the lives of others proved to be *one* way to deactivate unwanted partiality. I spent the time discovering all I could about these dear women. I asked who they were, where they came from, and what God was saying to them during this special time. I inquired how each had come to know Christ personally. Unavoidable questions were answered with reflections on the reality of Christ in my life, without "biting the bait" to talk about myself. As the luncheon ended and we prepared to leave the table, we shook hands, hugged and agreed that the Lord had truly blessed us. We were one in Christ. That fact makes us all special, and all joyful!

Where is the weak link in our speaking and doing His truth? According to James 2:10, "For whoever keeps the whole law and yet stumbles in one point, he has become guilty of all." We like to minimize our sin and maximize our goodness, don't we? But this passage about the seriousness of sin shakes us. Unchecked sin becomes rampant. Instead of dressing it up to look respectable, we are to have an unrelenting hostility toward it. If Jesus had to die for it, it is serious enough to confess, and be delivered from.

One phrase in verse eight will keep us from breaking down and showing partiality—"fulfill the royal law." The royal law is love. If we consistently and pure-heartedly love our neighbor, *all* neighbors, the "but" in verse nine need not follow. To have an attitude of personal favoritism is to waver in our attempt to have unconditional love for all.

But is there anything more difficult than trying to muster *feelings* of love toward a person who is downright unlovable? What sweet relief to discover that love is not a feeling. Love is an act of the will to accept, honor, and care for another in obedience to our Lord's command. We must be *willing* to let His Spirit of love be demonstrated through us as God reaches out to others—without respect of persons. God hates sin, but He loves sinners! We can be the same way. We can love the rich and poor, the lovely and unlovely, the dirty and clean, the adulterer and murderer as well as the self-righteous and partial.

Our next consideration is how to put shoe leather to a command that requires action to be received by another. A missionary to the city of Jerusalem discovered an "A-B-C" formula that has transformed my ability to love others. I have meditated upon it and taught it to others for the past six years. These A-B-C's of love are contained in Hannah Hurnard's book, *The Kingdom of Love* (Wheaton, IL: Tyndale House Pubs., 1975). A/Accepting (with joy). B/Bearing. C/Creative love thoughts.

These three ideas were revealed to me during a time when I wanted with all of my heart to *totally* reject several people who had wounded me deeply. It seemed impossible to *bear* the hurt and the consequences of their sins. In fact my life would be unalterably changed because of their transgressions. The open wounds might heal in time, but I knew there would be scars that periodically would remind me of the hurt. How could I muster a "creative love thought" toward people who obviously had imposed their own way on my life? "An eye for an eye—a tooth for a tooth." Now, that would have been a pleasure.

But by thinking that way, I was in bondage to bitterness, wrath and anger—a prisoner of grief, regret and wounded pride. I verbally confessed these sins as I read and re-read the A-B-C's, knowing they pointed to "the perfect law of liberty."

Trying to ignore my heartache, I reflected on what I knew to be true. First, I recognized that Jesus had accepted me as I was, loving the sinner, but hating the sin. He went to the cross before He was in the position to forgive. His message about redemption would have been worthless had He not become the sin-bearer. Furthermore, I reasoned that God had revealed innumerable love thoughts through His physical creation. The lilies, birds, stars, seas, shells, flowers, and trees—all demonstrated the infinite variety of His creativity. Even Scripture had defined God as *Creative Love.*

Therefore, if He lives in us, and we understand how to appropriate His power to fill and control us, we should *never* exhaust His love thoughts which He desires to impart and release through us.

As I meditated on A/Accepting (with joy), I learned that love is not a feeling. When we would like to see someone suffer, but instead choose to accept that person with joy regardless of whether he is sorry, we take the first step toward overcoming hurt.

When we decide to B/Bear the sins of others in obedience to Scripture, rejecting the pity parties, and rejecting the emotions that will entice us to be bitter, we take the second step toward freedom. Scripture points to Christ as our example:

> For what credit is there if, when you sin and are harshly treated, you endure it with patience? But if when you do what is right and suffer for it you patiently endure it, this finds favor with God. For you have been called for this purpose, since Christ also suffered for you, leaving you an example for you to follow in His steps, Who committed no sin, nor was any deceit found in his mouth: And while being reviled, He did not revile in return; while suffering, He uttered no threats, but kept entrusting Himself to Him who judges righteously; and He Himself bore our sins... (1 Peter 2:20-24a).

We should follow in *His* steps because love *bears* all things..." (1 Corinthians 13:7). While we cannot sustain another's sins in our body as He did on the cross, we *can* endure the hurt, pain, and consequences of another's sins toward us free of reviling and threatening—and *without* "gritting our teeth."

When we do, wounds, memories, facts and consequences no longer matter. God's C/Creative love thoughts release us to walk on a new plateau. The royal law of love is the most liberating truth we can grasp in God's "perfect law of liberty" because:

> Owe nothing to anyone except to love one another; for he who loves his neighbor has fulfilled the law (Romans 13:8).
>
> "By this all men will know that you are My disciples, if you have love for one another" (John 13:35).
>
> "This is My commandment, that you love one another, just as I have loved you. Greater love has no one than this, that one lay down his life for his friends" (John 15:12-13).
>
> "Truly, truly, I say to you, unless a grain of wheat falls into the earth and dies, it remains by itself alone; but if it dies, it bears much fruit. He who loves his life loses it; and he who hates his life in this world shall keep it to life eternal" (John 12:24-25).

The list of benefits could go on and on. As we fulfill the royal law by loving all people, there are *no* blessings not intended for us to experience and enjoy. Oh, so much is at stake here! As I counsel women who are crushed through adultery, divorce or a wayward child, and I see their desire to lash out, I *always* share the A-B-C's of love, assuring them that they have to be violating one or more of these principles or they would know *Christ's liberty.* To deliberately withhold love from a person is to be a "respecter of persons."

Fortunately, God's love has never depended upon its object. If it did, He could not love me or you. His affection rests upon the subject — Himself, for He *is* love! Love is the fruit of His Spirit. Since our love for others also is not contingent upon its object, is there anyone we cannot love for any reason? There should not be. Because we are even commanded to love our enemies, there can be no limits to His love.

Before asking you to identify a person you may have difficulty loving, let me answer a question I know you might be asking, "Do I have to spend time with someone who has repeatedly made life impossible?" If that someone is your mate, this method is not giving you a way "out"! You are one flesh with that person, and God desires the marriage to work more than you do! If we follow His royal law of love, God will have the freedom to work in any situation.

Not only will He give us love for our families and friends, but He will grant us strength to love our "enemies," such as the gossip, or the one who degrades us, or the one who argues and never earns our trust. God's Word gives us examples of people who had to deal with their enemies. David, for instance, would have been a fool to hang around Saul's wrath and spears! But he did honor his king, an act of love, and kept out of his way, an act of wisdom. He avoided harming Saul when he had opportunity and confessed his sin when he once made him look foolish. He did not withhold love. Jesus often avoided his enemies by associating with chosen people. While He was on earth, He did not entrust Himself to many because He knew that they were untrustworthy. He chose to spend quality time with Peter, James and John. He also worked patiently with the others of the 12 disciples. He was selective; but never exclusive! Passionately, He cried, "Come to Me, all who are weary. . . ."

Paul was blessed with Timothy, a disciple whom he chose. He also hand-picked Barnabas and Luke to co-labor with him. But he loved everyone in the churches and wrote them heart-felt prayers and exhortations — even the ones living in sin and error.

We all have been blessed with special friends, who are more

priceless than jewels, absolute treasures from God! A trustworthy confidant doesn't come along every day, but they're worth waiting for! However, no friendship should create such a "holy huddle" that others feel your love has limits, and your acceptance conditions. If this impression is given, they may think that they don't measure up. Always apply the A-B-C's rather than withholding love. Because Jesus has commanded us to love, and partiality is the antithesis of affection, we are to care for our neighbors, ourselves and our enemies.

The way of love is often a narrow path. Everyone I talk to is struggling with at least one relationship where they desire to be exclusive and partial. Are we willing to confess any "respect of persons" of which we might be guilty? Will we consent to be cleansed and quit short-circuiting God's love? It may be painful to admit that God loves our difficult adversary—but He does! To look down our noses at another person does not make us superior, it only reveals our evil thoughts. To hold a grudge does not inflict justified punishment for our pain, it only puts *us* in bondage.

Being partial to someone is like pouring a vial of poison into the Lord's cup of joy. That person permeates our emotions, our thought processes and our behavior patterns. And that paralyzes our walk in God's power. We must be willing to apply the A-B-C's of love to "trying" relationships. The desired response may not readily appear, but God will begin to "fine tune" our hearts.

Reflect and Act

Disobedience quenches joy. The commandments of Jesus have been given so that His joy might remain in us and that we might be full! There is no human relationship or sin committed against us that is worth being robbed of God's joy! No matter who the person is or what they've done, we *must* let Christ love them through us, so that we can experience His joy. Loving keeps us out of debt. "Owe nothing to anyone except to love one another; for he who loves his neighbor has fulfilled the law" (Romans 13:8).

> Search my heart, O God. You know where I have been critical, partial, exclusive, judgmental . . . You know where I am indebted to express LOVE, and have not done it. If

I am to owe NO man ANYTHING but love, I will need to
Accept _____

Bear _____

and extend **C**reative love thoughts toward _____

_____ .

Help me see "trying relationships" as opportunities to
learn about divine love. With your power and grace, I plan
to

Chapter 10

The Faith-Works Dilemma
James 2:14-26

14 What use is it my brethren, if a man says he has faith, but he has no works? Can that faith save him? 15 If a brother or sister is without clothing and in need of daily food, 16 and one of you says to them. "Go in peace, be warmed and be filled," and yet you do not give them what is necessary for *their* body, what use is that? 17 Even so faith, if it has not works, is dead, *being* by itself. 18 But someone may *well* say, "You have faith, and I have works; show me your faith without the works, and I will show you my faith by my works." 19 You believe that God is one. You do well; the demons also believe, and shudder. 20 But are you willing to recognize, you foolish fellow, that faith without works is useless? 21 Was not Abraham our father justified by works, when he offered up Isaac his son on the altar? 22 You see that faith was working with his works, and as a result of the works, faith was perfected; 23 and the Scripture was fulfilled which says, "AND ABRAHAM BELIEVED GOD, AND IT WAS RECKONED TO HIM AS RIGHTEOUSNESS," and he was called the friend of God. 24 You see that a man is justified by works, and not by faith alone. 25 And in the same way was not Rahab the harlot also justified by works, when she received the messengers and sent them out by another way? 26 For just as the body without *the* spirit is dead, so also faith without works is dead.

IF WE take 98 percent truth and sprinkle it with 2 percent error, what do we have? Simply more evidence that Satan is alive and well, and that religion is still his target. Satan has always done a masterful job of confusing issues in the church. He majors in taking truth and twisting it around until it becomes camouflaged error. The faith-works issue is one area where he has tried master-fully to entangle the Christian. James unmasks Satan's decep-tion in chapter 2, verses 14 through 20.

Churches are filled with people who are counting on good works to save them — the old "cart before the horse" routine. On the other hand, congregations have many people who declare their faith, but who reveal nothing in words or deeds to confirm their claim. This is the problem James refers to when he speaks of faith versus works.

The works-righteousness concept began in the garden of Eden when Adam and Eve tried to cover themselves with leaves. The Lord provided skin coverings for them which must have resulted from the shedding of blood. Only God could clothe them to stand in His presence. At this time, He instituted the plan of redemption ". . . without shedding of blood there is no forgiveness" (Hebrews 9:22).

Cain and Abel continued the battle between faith and works. While Abel was willing to bring a sheep to be offered as a blood sacrifice to God, his brother insisted on offering his good works — the crop he had harvested with his hands. Hebrews 11:4 assures us it was *faith* in God's system of redemption that made Abel acceptable in God's sight: "By faith Abel offered to God a better sacrifice than Cain, through which he obtained the testimony that he was righteous . . . ."

Adam and Eve evidently had been faithful to pass God's plan on to their children. One believed it and demonstrated his faith with works. The other did not believe and insisted on approaching and worshipping God on his own terms — with the fruit of *his* labor. Therefore, his works were not accepted.

The issue is not whether a person is involved in works. All "religious" people are doing works. The person with "saving faith" does works which are scriptural and which glorify God. His works flow out of a grateful heart. But the "Cains" in our churches are like the Jews of Christ's time. They go through the acts of wor-ship and works, but deny the need for a blood sacrifice for their sins in order to be accepted by the Father. We have talked to these "Cains" by the *hundreds,* and all sing a similar tune: "I don't believe a loving God will reject me when I've lived a good life, done the best I could and never hurt anyone." They are count-ing on their *works* to save them. They have "the cart before the horse!" First is their *works.* Next is faith *in* their *works.* But they have bypassed the *work* of the cross—Christ's shed blood for their sin. They would do well to analyze Ephesians 2:8, 9: "For by grace you have been saved through faith; and that not of yourselves, it is the gift of God; not as a result of works, that no one should boast."

What then of works? How do they fit into God's plan for man? As noted, the person with "saving faith" will be motivated by gratefulness to glorify God. That individual will search the Scriptures to find ways to please His Lord. Although the object of his faith is the blood sacrifice of Christ, he will move from that kind of faith to the outflowing type of faith described in Ephesians 2:10: "For we are His workmanship, created in Christ Jesus for good works, which God prepared beforehand, that we should walk in them."

We *are* intended, as Christians, to glorify God by our works. Our works become the external proof or evidence of our internal life in Him. And the one who *says* he has "saving faith," but who does not demonstrate it with scriptural acts, needs to examine his faith. He may be deceiving himself! James challenges professing believers to think twice about whether their faith is in fact "saving faith":

> What use is it, my brethren, if a man says he has faith, but he has no works? Can that faith save him? If a brother or sister is without clothing and in need of daily food, and one of you says to them, "Go in peace, be warmed and be filled," and yet you do not give them what is necessary for their body, what use is that? Even so faith, if it has no works, is dead, being by itself. But someone may well say, "You have faith, and I have works; show me your faith without the works, and I will show you my faith by my works." You believe that God is one. You do well; the demons also believe, and shudder. But are you willing to recognize, you foolish fellow, that faith without works is useless? (James 2:14-20)

Many who profess to have faith in God may possess nothing more than intellectual assent to His existence. James adds that even the demons acknowledge the existence of God. But you won't find them devoted to His glory, lordship and eternal plan to redeem mankind! You certainly won't see them subject to His ordinances and obedient to His holy Word. "Saving faith" will be demonstrated. There *will* be outward evidence of the inward life of Christ! We are known by what we profess to be and by the fruit we bear. When others see that our walk reflects our talk, they have confidence that we are "for real"—not a bunch of "hot air," given to "lip service," and not masquerading hypocrites. We are temples of the Living God, whose Spirit indwells us, motivating us to live, work and serve for His glory! John penned it well when he said:

> And by this we know that we have come to know Him, if we keep His commandments. The one who says, "I have come to know Him," and does not keep His commandments, is a liar, and the truth is not in him; but whoever keeps His word, in him the love of God has truly been perfected. By this we know that we are in Him (1 John 2:3-5).

To keep His commandments is to live a life of service and obedience. This is not an invitation to search the Scriptures and get involved in a few good works that particularly appeal to us. But as Jesus' mother so beautifully said, "Whatever He says to you, do it" (John 2:5). We don't pick and choose; we follow and obey. And if our faith is in the atoning work of Christ rather than in our works or in our faith, we will bear the evidence of His life and light. Faith without works is dead—lifeless, and lightless. In the Sermon on the Mount Jesus emphasized:

> "You are the light of the world. A city set on a hill cannot be hidden. Nor do men light a lamp, and put it under the peck-measure, but on the lampstand; and it gives light to all who are in the house. Let your light shine before men in such a way that they may see your good works, and glorify your Father who is in heaven" (Matthew 5:14-16).

It is comforting to know that our righteousness and acceptance are in Jesus. This frees us from the futile self-effort to earn our way into Heaven. Our deeds are not the basis of our security in Christ, but the evidence of it! James illustrates how the works of Abraham and Rahab reflected the light of the "saving faith" they had in their hearts:

> Was not Abraham our father justified by works, when he offered up Isaac his son on the altar? You see that faith was working with his works, and as a result of the works, faith was perfected; and the Scripture was fulfilled which says, "And Abraham believed God, and it was reckoned to Him as righteousness," and he was called the friend of God.

You see that a man is justified by works, and not by faith alone (James 2:21-24).

Notice the repetition of the word *see*. We should be able to see visible evidence of a man's "saving faith" by the works he does. God sees our hearts and knows if they are right with Him and spiritually alive. But man can look only on the outward appearance, so our works will be the visible evidence of a heart that is trusting in the sacrifice of Christ alone for eternal *life*. Rahab also was justified by her works:

> And in the same way was not Rahab the harlot also justified by works, when she received the messengers and sent them out by another way? For just as the body without the spirit is dead, so also faith without works is dead (James 2:25, 26).

Hebrews 11 has often been called "The Hall of Fame," as it lists the great men and women of faith who serve as our examples. And listed among them is the name of a harlot: "By faith Rahab the harlot did not perish along with those who were disobedient, after she had welcomed the spies in peace" (Hebrews 11:31). Her works demonstrated the faith she had in Jehovah. She would have been dead with the others had she not provided the visible evidence to God's people that she was to be counted among them!

In these verses, God is trying to rattle the cages of false security. He knows the churches are filled with people who are good at "talking" the Christian life, but there are no outward signs of Christ-honoring works in their "walk." They are spectators, but they are not in the battle. They profess, but do not possess.

Before I came to trust in Christ, I taught Sunday school, attended church, "believed" in God, and counted on the heavenly Father to look favorably on all I had done when the day of judgment came (if there truly was such a thing). I actually kept a list of all the the good works I had done in the pigeonhole desk in my living room. If something happened to me, I wanted to be sure an accurate obituary would remind everyone that my life *had* counted! People chuckle when I tell them that. They see the vanity of my ways and can't believe I would confess to such an "ego trip." But they agree with me that the reason I was determined not to go unnoticed is that down deep inside, we all want to know our lives count. My good works would have been approved by my fellow man, and I was sure God would not only accept, but surely reward my well-meaning efforts.

What a rude awakening when Ephesians 2:8, 9 finally got through to me, and I was "saved through faith" in the work of Christ. Being faced with the truth was such a jolt, that I did what many others have done — let the pendulum swing from one extreme to the other. For the first few years, my time was devoted to Bible study, prayer, witnessing, teaching and obeying the command to make disciples. Feeding the hungry and clothing the naked seemed to be something the charitable organizations were taking care of well enough. However, they left out the gospel, and I couldn't condone clothing and feeding a body only to send it down the road to hell. They could count me out!

But as time passed, the Lord patiently began to show me the Christian's responsibility both to witness to God's salvation and meet temporal needs. The picture came into focus the week before Christmas this year. In our Bible study, we had been studying Luke, and I was preparing a lecture for chapter 10 when Jeanne called. She and a neighbor had had an ongoing discussion about "faith and works" that repeatedly challenged Jeanne to take action. And she had finally figured out what to do. Hesitantly, she asked if the leadership of the Creative Living Bible Study would be interested in sponsoring a needy family over the holidays. She had access to names of people who were destitute due to crisis situations, and several women in her church wanted to get involved.

Immediately, I thought of our study in Luke. In chapter 10, Jesus not only sent out the 70, two by two, to harvest souls for eternity, but He also told the parable of the good Samaritan who had stopped on the roadside to meet the needs of one man. This was after the "religious" priest and Levite had passed by the man, "not wanting to get involved." The responsibility to do both was before us.

Once we agreed not to limit God, we telephoned all 300 women in the group to tell them about "Operation Good Samaritan." They came two days later with canned goods, clothing (clean and sized), and wrapped gifts labeled for men, women and children. Jeanne saw God work mightily as other organizations like ours eagerly joined in, sharing her enthusiasm. God stretched our faith, as 17 families' needs were met.

But the lesson hit even closer to home. Following the lecture, I went into the visitor's class to meet the eight or ten first-timers. We discussed the history of our study, looked at the material, and made an effort to get to know one another. As our time came to a close, a young woman burst into tears. She related how she had wanted to leave the sanctuary, fill her car with the canned goods we had unloaded in the foyer, and leave, because there was no food at home. Having had recent surgery, she could not return to work immediately, and a series of circumstances had left her with no compensation. This woman was a nurse with a job waiting for her. But for now, she had to feed herself and two children, and she didn't have one dollar to her name.

Could this be? Right in the midst of our affluent Philadelphia suburb? Yes, it certainly could. Our mighty God had brought us an "object lesson." She cried, "I heard your message and I know I should listen to you tell me how I can know Jesus, but I'm so desperate I can't think. Are you for real? Do you people really care?" The rest of the visitors had heard the message, too. As she talked, their purses spontaneously opened and money was passed to her. She was overwhelmed by the compassion, and the tears flowed freely.

When we assured her that food would follow, and that we would include her family in the "Christmas" we were organizing for others, *then* she was open to hear! We prayed for God to quiet her heart and open her understanding. Patsy passed out the Four Spiritual Laws and gave everyone an opportunity to accept Jesus in silent prayer, if they had not done so.

As this young woman left that day, she assured me that she had received Christ. She said she understood that our gifts were temporary, but that His was eternal. We later learned that at home she shared Christ with her two children using The Good News Comic Book. She told them that God loved them *so much,* He had sent her to some of His children for help — and that they had helped abundantly!

The Lord desires us to unite our willingness to speak of faith with our determination to be involved with good works. If we truly do have the "horse" in front, there will be a "cart" in the rear! The faith that saves, *works!*

Perhaps you have heard the little rhyme:
Only one life — 'twill soon be past.
Only what's done, for Christ will last.

That rhyme has floated into my mind many times when I have been trying to evaluate my priorities and set goals. We should do all in the name of Christ — from making our beds to folding laundry. However, I am concerned about Christians who expend great amounts of energy on community projects where proclaiming Christ is not welcomed. If our works only satisfy our sense of accomplishment, they will amount to nothing in eternity.

Reflect and Act

In order to check your own horse and cart, ask yourself, "What am I doing for Christ's sake?"

Now ask yourself, "So what? Will it count for Eternity?"

The Horse: I received Christ and knew I had saving faith

The Cart: Out of a heart of gratitude and a desire to glorify God *alone,* these works are intended to demonstrate my saving faith:

Chapter 11

It's Tongue-Taming Time
James 3:1-12

LET not many *of you* become teachers, my brethren, knowing that as such we shall incur a stricter judgment. 2 For we all stumble in many *ways*. If anyone does not stumble in what he says, he is a perfect man, able to bridle the whole body as well. 3 Now if we put the bits into the horses' mouths so that they may obey us, we direct their entire body as well. 4 Behold, the ships also, though they are so great and are driven by strong winds, are still directed by a very small rudder, wherever the inclination of the pilot desires. 5 So also the tongue is a small part of the body, and *yet* it boasts of great things. Behold, how great a forest is set aflame by such a small fire! 6 And the tongue is a fire, the *very* world of iniquity; the tongue is set among our members as that which defiles the entire body, and sets on fire the course of *our* life and is set on fire by hell. 7 For every species of beasts and birds, of reptiles and creatures of the sea, is tamed, and has been tamed by the human race. 8 But no one can tame the tongue; *it is* a restless evil *and* full of deadly poison. 9 With it we bless *our* Lord and Father: and with it we curse men, who have been made in the likeness of God; 10 from the same mouth come *both* blessing and cursing. My brethren, these things ought not to be this way. 11 Does a fountain send out from the same opening *both* fresh and bitter *water*? 12 Can a fig tree, my brethren, produce olives, or a vine produce figs? Neither *can* salt water produce fresh.

MOST THINGS that are powerful have the capacity for good or evil—the atom, explosives, drugs, sex, weapons, the intellect, emotions, and so on. According to James, the tongue is among the *most* powerful instruments we have at our disposal. With this power comes the potential to delight or destroy.

James, chapter 3, begins with a warning to teachers: "Let not many of you become teachers, my brethren, knowing that as such we shall incur a stricter judgment. For we all stumble in many ways" (James 3:1, 2a). As James approaches the subject of our powerful tongues, he issues a warning to those who accept the awesome challenge and responsibility of teaching the Word of God. Knowing the influence a teacher can have on a student, he reminds them of their accountability to God. It is a staggering thing to think that the error of our thoughts or the inconsistency of our lives might lead someone astray, and that Bible teachers will one day see God review and judge these deeds.

It is true that in many things we all stumble. God knows we are not perfect in the sense of "sinless perfection." But He warns us to be mature, stable, consistent examples of walking in the light of His Word, if we dare to teach it. A Bible teacher should be a person whose heart is harnessed with the Lord and who is willing to respond to God's leading in every area of his life. As James points out, "If anyone does not stumble in what he says, he is a perfect man, able to bridle the whole body as well" (James 3:2b). This Christian reveals his walk with the Lord by the inoffensive way he speaks and by his self-control. Since self-discipline is a fruit of God's Holy Spirit, this is the description of a mature, Spirit-*controlled* person. Every Christian would like to be this kind of person, and we all could learn from this type of teacher.

If we know of an area of our lives where we do not have victory over our bodies, we may conclude that the weakness has probably been caused by our tongue. There have been times we knew that what we said was not edifying, loving or glorifying to God. If we are honest, we will admit that our nasty little tongues often say things we later regret. They reveal the "unbridled" condition of our heart.

The tongue is not something we should befriend or defend, but an instrument that we should understand and yield to God's control. James compares the tongue to two things: the bit in a horse's mouth, and the helm of a ship:

> Now if we put the bits into the horses' mouths so that they may obey us, we direct their entire body as well.
> Behold, the ships also, though they are so great and are driven by strong winds, are still directed by a very small rud-

der, wherever the inclination of the pilot desires.

So also the tongue is a small part of the body, and yet it boasts of great things. (James 3:3-5a).

Whenever we see the word *behold* in Scripture, we need to think for a moment about what is being said. In the Greek, the word means to look over carefully, giving more than a casual glance. The word behold in these verses flags the fact that our tongues are being compared to two tiny instruments that greatly influence the objects they guide. We must understand that our tongues, if unbridled, will contribute to unchecked bodily passions and activities. If we fail to control the tongue, we will be out of control, victims of fleshly desires that we are helpless to overcome.

Once we have recognized to what extent our tongues can be destructive, perhaps we won't be so quick to defend them. We will instead cry out for God to harness and bridle this unruly power!

There are five characteristics of the tongue explained in verses 6 through 10, which James says are reasons for its destructive power. First, the nature of the tongue is "the very world of iniquity." Second, its influence is to "defile the *entire* body." Third, it has a continuing effect because it "sets on fire the *course* of our life." Fourth, it is affiliated with hell—proving its anti-God, pro-Satan source. And fifth, it is unpredictable. "Out of the same mouth come both blessing and cursing."

The character of the tongue is a fire which consumes, destroys, burns and scars. It leaves charred memories of what once was, but cannot be restored. It devastates. Again the word *behold* alerts us to read the revelation carefully:

> Behold, how great a forest is set aflame by such a small fire! And the tongue is a fire, the very world of iniquity; the tongue is set among our members as that which defiles the entire body, and sets on fire the course of our life, and is set on fire by hell.
>
> . . . With it we bless our Lord and Father; and with it we curse men, who have been made in the likeness of God; from the same mouth come both blessing and cursing. My brethren, these things ought not to be this way.
>
> Does a fountain send out from the same opening both fresh and bitter water?
>
> Can a fig tree, my brethren, produce olives, or a vine pro-

duce figs? Neither can salt water produce fresh (James 3:5b, 6, 9-12).

Here is disclosed the vile character, insidious influence, on-going, uncontrollable effect and hellish source attributed to our tiny, wagging, little tongues.

Everything in nature is consistent. We can expect a fountain, fig tree or vine to consistently "do its thing." Nature yields to the authority of God. But since the fall, mankind has been predictably unpredictable, and it is evidenced by the inconsistency of what we say!

Sadly when our mouths utter both blessing and cursing— like any bitter water added to sweet, the sour *always* overrules and permeates that which is clear and good. If someone remarked about a person, "She has a sweet side that many admire, but I think she's childish and shallow," the next time we saw that person we would probably think of "childish and shallow" rather than the "sweet side."

Our words can hurt deeply. For years I was involved in several Bridge clubs. While I enjoyed the game marginally, the real stimulation of these evenings was in catching up on the *gossip*. Sodom and Gomorrah had nothing on our little American suburb! I didn't *dare* miss the meeting because I might become the object of idle talk, if I were not there. As the Scripture explains, life and death come from the tongue and flattery often precedes the wounds.

> Death and life are in the power of the tongue,
> And those who love it will eat its fruit (Proverbs 18:21).
> Like charcoal to hot embers and wood to fire,
> So is a contentious man to kindle strife.
> The words of a whisperer are like dainty morsels,
> [The words of a talebearer are as wounds (KJV)] (Proverbs 26:21,22a).
>
> He who hates disguises it with his lips,
> But he lays up deceit in his heart.
> When he speaks graciously, do not believe him (Proverbs 26:24, 25a).
>
> A lying tongue hates those it crushes.
> And a flattering mouth works ruin (Proverbs 26:28).

Men have *died* for saying the wrong thing! And homes have crumbled into ashes over the irretrievable words that set them ablaze! I know, because mine almost did!

"I wish I had never come home!" Those words stung the air as I looked at the man in the overcoat standing inside the living room door. I had opened my mouth and done it again! While my husband was working all day and finishing law school at night, I was cooped up with two toddlers in a small house with no access to a car. Pressures mounted all day, and there was no adult to discuss them with. I knew I should welcome my mate, help him relax and unwind from *his* hectic day and then eventually talk through any problems we needed to share. But I was "up to my ears" with this existence, and my tongue was determined to let *him* know it!

"I wish I had never come home!" The echo of his words made me realize that our marriage was in trouble. He began to come home less and less. Why couldn't I get on top of these "explosions" that made our home so tense? I blamed myself. Every time I would strike the match with my fiery complaint, he would fan the spark with his "hot air." We were a "dynamic duo," *playing with fire* and in the exact circumstances described in Proverbs:

> A fool's lips bring strife,
> And his mouth calls for blows.
> A fool's mouth is his ruin,
> And his lips are the snare of his soul. (Proverbs 18:6, 7).
> It is better to live in a corner of a roof,
> Than in a house shared with a contentious woman.
> It is better to live in a desert land,
> Than with a contentious and vexing woman (Proverbs 21:9, 19).

Christ has reigned in our home for 11 years, and I now have a husband who can't wait to come home.

As our pastor preached it one day in church, "What we think of others in our hearts will eventually be expressed in our words. Look around the sanctuary. Think of all the things you have said about those around you, though they probably don't know it. If any words have been unkind or unloving, think of those words wounding that person. Imagine blood dripping from each inflicted wound. Think of the time it will take for the wound to heal and imagine the scars that will be left."

Knowing how catty and cruel people can be, it was easy to imagine what others might be thinking, if they were actually doing what he suggested. Suddenly, I saw an acquaintance sitting in the pew across the aisle. It had been difficult to accept *her* the way she was. Through the spirit of discernment, I knew that God could use *her* more if she'd change a few glaring, obvious ways. Of course, I had discussed these matters with a friend — so that we could pray for *her*. It was comforting to know my friend agreed with my evaluation of *her*.

All I could see was the back of her head as we worshipped God together and received instruction from His Word. But from where I sat, she was mortally wounded and bleeding profusely. God had shed light on the wounds I had inflicted, and it broke my heart. I was like those:

> Who have sharpened their tongue like a sword.
> They aimed bitter speech as their arrow. (Psalms 64:3).
> There is one who speaks rashly like the thrusts of a sword,
> But the tongue of the wise brings healing (Proverbs 12:18).

Like a power weapon, our tongues have the capacity to destroy, and we are masters at hitting our targets!

Our bitter words become arrows that destroy joy.

"I hate you!" "She really is stupid!" "He makes me sick!" "You should never count on her!"

"Have you heard about . . . ?" "Don't tell anyone, but you ought to know . . . " "This mustn't get around, but we ought to be praying for . . . ."

Sometimes even our good advice and well-intended words can come from the pit and mislead others. Therefore, it is important to know the principles of God's Word as we instruct or encourage others. "Be diligent to present yourself approved to God as a workman who does not need to be ashamed, handling accurately the word of truth" (2 Timothy 2:15). An example of someone who used misplaced words would be Peter. Out of the depths of human love and wisdom he tried to argue with the Lord concerning His impending death:

> From that time Jesus Christ began to show His disciples that He must go to Jerusalem, and suffer many things from the elders and chief priests and scribes, and be killed, and be raised up on the third day.
> And Peter took Him aside and began to rebuke Him, saying, "God forbid it, Lord! This shall never happen to You."
> But He turned and said to Peter, "Get behind Me, Satan!

You are a stumbling block to Me; for you are not setting your mind on God's interests, but man's" (Matthew 16:21-23).

We have discussed thus far the destructive power inherent in the tongue. But the problem is magnified when we discover the frailty of human effort to control that tongue! James exposes that inability:

> For every species of beasts and birds, of reptiles and creatures of the sea, is tamed, and has been tamed by the human race. But no one can tame the tongue; it is a restless evil and full of deadly poison . . . .My brethren, these things ought not to be this way (James 3:7, 8, 10b).

J. B. Phillips calls the tongue an unruly, restless evil which is "always liable to break out!" — a run-away horse! We have all known secrets we wanted to tell. There is a restless feeling until we can rationalize a reason for telling. It is a riotous ill, full of deadly poison. One victim, for example, left a suicide note which simply read, "They said . . . ." How many bitter words have poisoned our minds, our morals and our dreams?

We may want to speak only what is kind, but our tongues defy human restraint. When God said, "The tongue can *no* man tame," He *meant* it! We can hate it; we can bite it; we can lament over its outbursts and swear we'll *never* let it happen again . . . but we will never control it!

Since our tongues are potentially destructive and cannot be tamed, we must face the consequences of our words. Jesus told us the price we will pay:

> "And I say to you, that every careless word that men shall speak, they shall render account for it in the day of judgment" (Matthew 12:36).

We are responsible for *every* word we speak. Many Christians tolerate areas of defeat in their lives. They defend, rather than face up to their poisonous enemy. They are trying to control something that is beyond their control. It is similar to playing with a snake whose bite has no cure.

Actually, the wagging tongue is nothing more than a "red flare" pointing to a deeper problem. The root of the matter is the condition of the heart.

Jesus said, our tongues are connected to our hearts:

> "You brood of vipers, how can you, being evil, speak what is good? For the mouth speaks out of that which fills the heart" (Matthew 12:34).
> "You hypocrites, rightly did Isaiah prophesy of you, saying,
> 'This people honors Me with their lips,
> But their heart is far away from Me'
> "But the things that proceed out of the mouth come from the heart, and those defile the man. For out of the heart come evil thoughts, murders, adulteries, fornications, thefts, false witness, slanders" (Matthew 15:7, 8, 18, 19).

This list of actions, thoughts, and words shouldn't alarm us if we know that our hearts are "deceitful and desperately sick" as revealed in Jeremiah 17:9. Our deceptive hearts mislead us into thinking that our motives are pure and our words justified, when often they aren't. We are content to live with our "blind spots" and masterfully apply the Christian life like makeup. But our lips *do* betray us. We may not hear our words revealing a striving heart—but others do. And the words we say dim the witness of the Christian walk which we profess.

If we ask the Lord to search our hearts, He is willing to reveal our blind spots, cleanse us of sin and cause us to walk in His statutes. "For it is God who is at work in you, both to will and to work for His good pleasure. Do all things without grumbling or disputing" (Philippians 2:13, 14). As always, the solution is Jesus. We *must* allow Christ to reign in our hearts. We could learn these lessons more quickly if we would not support our unbridled actions, our undisciplined habits, our unchecked emotions, our unrestrained tongues or our unruly hearts.

It is only when we use the tongue to *delight,* that we capture the joy of Christianity. This is achieved by positively proclaiming our own salvation:

> "The Word is near you, in your mouth and in your heart" —that is, the word of faith which we are preaching, that if you confess with your mouth Jesus as Lord, and believe in your heart that God raised Him from the dead, you shall be saved; for with the heart man believes, resulting in righteousness, and with the mouth he confesses, resulting in salvation (Romans 10:8-10).

The tongue *is* connected to the heart! We begin to delight God as we confess our faith and declare His righteousness to others. "The fruit of the righteous is a tree of life, And he who is wise wins souls" (Proverbs 11:30). The result of our confession will be our opportunity to share the gospel of Christ, "...the power of God for salvation..." (Romans 1:16).

My husband took to witnessing like a duck takes to water! I was more reluctant in that area, having to overcome the "what will the neighbors think?" syndrome. Our children have grown up hearing about the people we have led to receive Christ, and the joy of seeing their lives changed. Just how much influence our witnessing has had was made evident one evening, several winters ago, when Dave took our son, David, to his piano lesson. On their way home they stopped for gasoline. David sat in the car watching "a real cool man, with a flat green hat," happily greeting the customers as they pulled up for service. Suddenly, he turned to his dad and queried, "Dad, do you think that nice man knows Jesus?"

Daddy was not "tracking" with son when he answered, "I don't know, but we've got to get home."

David persisted. "But it only takes a few minutes to share Christ, Dad. Do you have any Four Spiritual Laws?"

Dave checked his pockets and the glove compartment. There were no booklets. He tried to persuade David that it was bitter cold and the man was probably eager to get back inside the station.

But David would not relent. "It would be much better for him to stand in the cold for a few minutes if it would keep him out of the heat of hell for eternity." *Now* Daddy was thinking on the same level!

When the attendant came to the window, Dave rolled it down and spoke: "My son and I have been sitting here talking, and he is very interested in knowing if you are a Christian."

"Sir, I know who the Lord is; I have heard about Jesus. But I have never given my life to Him. I'm awfully dirty. There is a lot I'd have to clean up before *I* could come to Jesus."

Dave assured him that he also had been "awfully dirty"— but he had discovered it was a "come as you are party." He described how Christ had died on the cross to pay the penalty for his sins and how Christ had "cleaned up his life" since he had received Him. After more words of explanation, this "real cool man with a flat green hat" said, "Sir, I *would* like to pray to receive Christ." And with that, he disappeared from sight!

Had he retreated to the warmth of the filling station? No, he had dropped to his knees beside the car, remove his hat, bowed his head, and was waiting for Dave to lead him in prayer! With the neon lights glaring and intersection traffic whirling around them, this man's heart became linked with the God of the universe!

"Thank you for taking time to talk with me," were his parting words.

When Dave and David got home, David burst through the front door with, "Mom! Tonight I led my first person to Christ!" Certainly, this child's persistence and sense of urgency for the man's soul had caused the words to come. "There is joy in the presence of the angels of God over one sinner who repents" (Luke 15:10). That evening, we joined in the angel's celebration! A week later, when they stopped again to get gas, they found him beaming and eager to accept booklets to help him grow in his new faith.

Think of the person or people who loved you enough to take time to tell you how to know Christ personally. Their tongues were used as instruments of God to bring you His good news. As in Ephesians 4:29, their voice was used to edify:

> Let no unwholesome word proceed from your mouth, but only such a word as is good for edification according to the need of the moment, that it may give grace to those who hear.

God will never ask us to do something that He will not empower us to do. It is true that our tongues are an untamable, poisonous fire, erupting from the hiding place of the unbridled heart. But it is also true that the harnessed heart with Jesus at the helm will direct our tongues to be instruments of peace, encouragement, edification and comfort. The church needs joy-filled words, not darts and arrows or wounds that leave us crippled!

The Christian who *has* a controlled tongue is a *marked person*. He has the mark of the supernatural on him. He is noticeably different from what James 3 describes.

Jesus was such a man:

Then I said,
"Woe is me, for I am ruined!
Because I am a man of unclean lips,
And I live among a people of unclean lips;
For my eyes have seen the King, the Lord of hosts" (Isaiah 6:5).

Who committed no sin, nor was any deceit found in His mouth" (1 Peter 2:22).

Christians, it's tongue-taming time! It's time we honestly evaluate if the one who had *no* guile in His mouth is truly at the helm. If we know that we have *never* offended with our words and that there are *no* undisciplined areas in our body, we have probably reached the limit of spiritual maturity. However, most of us need to think carefully on Colossians 3:15-17:

And let the peace of Christ *rule in your hearts* and be thankful. Let the word of Christ richly dwell within you, with all wisdom teaching and admonishing one another with psalms and hymns and spiritual songs, singing with thankfulness in your hearts to God. And whatever you do in word or deed, do all in the name of the Lord Jesus, giving thanks through Him to God the Father.

Reflect and Act

The following exercise will help determine what we are saying that needs to be confessed as sin. For one week, begin each day by praying, "Lord, *everything* I say today is meant to glorify You. I will speak with the authority of Your name and give You the credit for what I've said. As You sit at the helm of my heart, control my tongue like the horses' bit or the ship's rudder."

As you speak during the day, if there is the *slightest* tinge of conviction, repeat quietly, "Jesus, You get the credit for what I just said. I said it 'in the name of the Lord.'" If you can whisper that quietly, and it rings true in your heart, your words have glorified Him. If you utter it and your heart condemns you, confess your sin.

If approached correctly, the tongue can be a gauge to discover areas where our hearts have deceived us. When we quit befriending and defending it, God will tame and transform this restless, unruly member of our body. It's tongue-taming time—today, tomorrow and *every* day that God gives us to speak as His ambassadors.

God, forgive me for being predisposed to side with these:
(identify and list)
    unbridled actions

    unbridled habits

    unbridled emotions

    unbridled words toward

    unbridled heart attitudes

Thank you for the opportunities you have given or will
give me to:
    encourage

    witness

    comfort

Convict me when necessary. Remind me to ask, "Did I
say that in the name of Jesus, wanting Him to get credit
for that remark?" Harness and tame my tongue and heart,
since I am helpless to do so. Amen.

Chapter 12

Friend of the World —Enemy of God James 3:13—4:5

13 Who among you is wise and understanding? Let him show by his good behavior his deeds in the gentleness of wisdom. 14 But if you have bitter jealousy and selfish ambition in your in your heart, do not be arrogant and *so* lie against the truth. 15 This wisdom is not that which comes down from above, but is earthly, natural, demonic. 16 For where jealousy and selfish ambition exist, there is disorder and every evil thing. 17 But the wisdom from above is first pure, then peaceable, gentle, reasonable, full of mercy and good fruits, unwavering, without hypocrisy. 18 And the seed whose fruit is righteousness is sown in peace by those who make peace.

Things to Avoid

4 WHAT is the source of quarrels and conflicts among you? Is not the source your pleasures that wage war in your members? 2 You lust and do not have; *so* you commit murder. And you are envious and cannot obtain; *so* you fight and quarrel. You do not have because you do not ask. 3 You ask and do not receive, because you ask with wrong motives, so that you may spend *it* on your pleasures. 4 You adulteresses, do you not know that friendship with the world is hostility toward God? Therefore whoever wishes to be a friend of the world makes himself an enemy of God. 5 Or do you think that the Scripture speaks to no purpose: "He jealously desires the Spirit which He has made to dwell in us"?

DO YOU know someone who has been deeply hurt by an adulterous mate? If so, you have seen the anguish, grief, pain —

perhaps anger and bitterness— that accompany such a blow. Because intimacy has been defiled, there is rejection, loss, and broken trust. The problem is an old one, and God has repeatedly used the example of intimacy in marriage to draw an analogy of our closeness to Him. We are the bride, and He is the bridegroom.

There are some harsh words in James 4:4 which almost startle the believer:

> You adulteresses, do you not know that friendship with
> the world is hostility toward God? Therefore whoever wishes
> to be a friend of the world makes himself an enemy of God.

If this accusation came anywhere but from the Word of God, we would call it mud slinging. God labels "worldliness" or friendship with the world, as adulterated love or *spiritual* adultery. It simply means that we are allowing our love for something or someone other than God to satisfy our longings, receive our affections, and be a prime source of our pleasure.

The Word assures us in Exodus 20:5 and James 4:5 that God is a *jealous* God! He loves us with such passion that He cannot bear to see us flirting with or indulging in rival loves. His first commandment reminds us to love Him with all our heart, soul and mind. He is to be first and foremost. Yet at times, we get so "caught up in the world" that a casual observer might overlook our identity with Him altogether. If the people we meet were asked to guess what was the first love in our lives, would they think that it was God?

Eight centuries before Christ was born, God's people so grieved Him through rejection that He painstakingly proclaimed the message of spiritual adultery through the life of His prophet, Hosea. Hosea was a man of God who willingly submitted to God's plan—to live as an *object lesson* for God's people. Humbling himself before God, he obediently took Gomer, a harlot, to be his wife. She bore him two children and then returned to her old ways. Surely he was humiliated and hurt. And he had to rear his children without their mother!

Sin is a downward spiral. When Gomer ended up in a slave market, the Lord once again gave instruction to Hosea. He was to buy her back and restore her to the place of dignity in his home as wife and mother. In brokenness and humility this prophet was ready to be God's instrument to bring His message to the people:

> Harlotry, wine and new wine take away the understanding. My people consult their wooden idol . . . For a spirit of harlotry has led them astray, and they have played the harlot, departing from their god (Hosea 4:11, 12).
>
> They are all adulterers (7:4).
>
> Return, O Israel, to the Lord your God. For you have stumbled because of your iniquity (14:1).
>
> I will heal their apostasy, I will love them freely (14:4).

Can you imagine the intensity of anguish in Hosea's heart as he proclaimed this word to Israel? The message pulsated with emotion through its accusation, exhortation, warning and heartfelt pleading. Hosea *knew* the anguish of rejection and the cost of redemptive love. He had learned experientially of God's heart and he cried: "You adulteresses—return!"

God used this analogy to illustrate His pain and sorrow when He watches us willfully put Him in the back of our minds and let other people or things crowd out His pre-eminence. Although it could be immoral activity, often it will be our work, our mates or children, even Christian service, that will crowd Him into a corner of our hearts.

One way we can make a quick check on ourselves to see if we might be guilty of spiritual adultery is to evaluate the time we spend with God. Whether we call it quiet time, prayer time, Bible study and prayer—the question is: "Do we spend quality, consistent time alone with the Lord? We may *say* He's first in our life and fool ourselves, but we don't fool Him! God wants us to meditate upon His Word day and night. He desires for us to worship and praise Him and have lingering fellowship in His presence. This takes discipline and determination. Too often, we breathlessly acknowledge that He's there as we run off to our activity. But we keep appointments at the hair dresser and make it to scheduled meetings! The Lord is "stood up" by our adulterated love. Imagine—minimizing an audience with the King! We must have our heads screwed on backwards if we keep letting that happen.

Many respectable activities take precedence over our time with the Lord. The Sunday golfer will tell you how easy it is to worship God and appreciate nature as he walks eighteen holes. Jogging on the beach or gardening cannot be substitutes for church. God said we must not forsake the assembling of ourselves together.

At a recent Bible study, the young teacher described "friendship with the world" and how it leads to unrighteousness. Without giving the title of the show, he spoke about the funniest, wittiest, cleverest TV program on the air. Several people guessed it right away. He pointed out that the show was so well produced that the viewer couldn't help but laugh — even though all of the humor condoned *unrighteousness!* Everyone laughed and agreed. I sat there biting my tongue, wanting to ask, "If you know that the humor will make you laugh at the things that grieve God — *why* are you watching it?" To be a friend of the world is to be the enemy of God. Are we flirting with and even enjoying the world's humor that condones unrighteousness?

We might stop and examine the foothold that "things" have on us. Could we walk away from our home tonight, watch it disappear in flames and still praise the Lord? I've seen two friends do that in the last six months. Mary Sue and John stood barefooted in the snow with their four children and their dog at 2 a.m. praising God as their beautiful home was gutted by flames. They had beautiful furniture that had been accumulated during more than 20 years of marriage, and they wore good clothes. Everything was destroyed, but God protected the family album which they found on a charred table in the remains of their living room. They stepped out in faith to discover how mighty and loving the body of Christ can be when given an opportunity to rally in crisis.

My assistant, Janee, had met a friend for coffee at the end of a busy evening. So, it was 10:30 when she drove down her country dirt driveway. But this night was different. Two fire trucks ahead of her and four fire trucks behind raced to her adorable country cottage which was lit up like a torch. This precious woman, quite skilled in sewing, had made a good part of her elegant wardrobe. She *lost everything!* But her voice was steady and full of praise as she related how much worse it could have been. She saw the Lord's protecting hand in it and knew He would continue to supply her needs. She was considering it all joy, even though she realized that she would have to work through the pangs of "loss."

These friends learned to hold loosely the cloak of materialism. They still enjoy "things," and they will replace much of what the fires destroyed. But since the Lord is the source of their satisfaction, affection and pleasure, they are able to keep walking in His joy. We might ask the question of ourselves, is there any "thing" I am grasping with all my might for fear the Lord will grab it away? If the answer was yes, it spells "friendship with the world."

As these *things* take precedence over God, it will soon be evidenced in our relationships with others. To operate by the world's system is to return to the self-centered assumption that *our* gratification is essential. *Our* world revolves around *our* opinions and having *our* way, preferably without interruption. When others threaten our plans, we react. James notes that spiritual adultery leads to a disordered life:

> Who among you is wise and understanding? Let him show by his good behavior his deeds in the gentleness of wisdom. But if you have bitter jealousy and selfish ambition in your heart, do not be arrogant and so lie against the truth. This wisdom is not that which comes down from above, but is earthly, natural, demonic. For where jealousy and selfish ambition exist, there is disorder and every evil thing (James 3:13-16).

In James 1 we were promised divine wisdom if we would only ask in faith. But after all the admonitions about partiality, faith without works, and the tongue, it seems time to take a test. Are we truly drawing upon heavenly wisdom, or have we subtly slipped back into the "world's way" of thinking without even realizing it? Though we are involved in many works and are living a good life, the proof of the pudding comes after the word *but* in chapter 3, verse 14: "But if you have bitter jealousy and selfish ambition *in your heart,* do not be arrogant and so lie against the truth."

Envy and strife are emotions caused by self-seeking aspirations. They are rooted in the heart and our words will eventually betray us. We may find ourselves putting others down, criticizing, complaining, and insisting on expressing our own opinion. Egotistic desire is simply *pride,* the root cause of all jealousy and contention.

The Word unmasks pride as the reason for envy and strife. This does not mean pride plus a good reason for our opinion, or pride and an inferiority complex, or pride and unrealized expectations, or pride and hurt feelings—but pride *only!* The writer of Proverbs stated it well: "Only by pride cometh contention: but with the well advised is wisdom" (Proverbs 13:10 KJV).

Often we will experience inner turmoil when we don't approve of a person's current behavior. On the other hand, we envy those we truly admire.

Somewhere in our lives, we can find a person or persons who cause us to strive in our heart. We sense conflict when we hear or see something about them, or try to relate to them. If this is the case, we must accept that *pride* is our *only* problem, — not the other individual. There may be truth in our opinion, and rationale in our reasoning; but if it has produced strife, it is the sin of *pride* — and must be confessed.

This is a painful process. I know it well. There is nothing that produces so much anguish as the process of shifting from: "It's their fault . . . I have good reason . . . " to "It's my *pride* — insidious, despicable and monstrous." In fact, I learned this firsthand as I struggled to write this chapter. I typed it out, based on the lecture notes from the Bible study. When my dear husband, who is my number one critic, read it, he didn't like it. He said it was dry, mechanical, and impersonal — without examples and stories. Did I detect a twinge of striving in my stomach? I'm convinced that striving, envy, and contention *do* affect us physically. It had taken me all day to write the draft — and I *was* disappointed. He *had* interrupted my progress toward a goal. As I lay quietly in our bed that night, I began to think. *Wasn't the purpose of this criticism to help me? Couldn't I handle criticism?* Once I confessed sin rather than disappointment, I was ready to tackle the typewriter again.

It's easier to face pride if you don't have to come against it alone. My friend Patsy called one day and we began to share. Patsy is the dear with the tear who said she wanted to become a "mighty oak." She and her husband came to know Christ through our ministry, and he left advertising so they could work with us full time.

As we talked, I did something I seldom do. I told her of the struggle I had been going through in several areas with my own mate, and how I was painfully having to rethink all that I was trying to write about envying and strife. She assured me that she would be praying for me and reminded me of what a dear, fine man I have. Then she asked if she could make *her* "true confession."

Through sweet tears mingled with laughter and understanding, we discussed a struggle she had gone through in recent months over *envying* me. While she reaffirmed her love for me, she described the terrible, awful feelings that would come over her when she thought of my energy level. She marveled that I could paint a room between 10 p.m. and 2 a.m., dash off an oil painting to go over the fireplace, and then go back to the typewriter or out to teach a Bible study. We call it "ten ball-bouncing," which is okay, till your timing gets off.

Finally, this dear friend had worked through the process of realizing that she mustn't compare herself to *anyone*. She understood that *pride* was at the root of her emotions, and she expressed how dreadful it had been to find herself capable of jealousy toward someone she loved and considered an intimate friend.

As Patsy and I talked about our mutual desire to see one another grow and bear fruit, and our desire to edify each other, I began to see that our envy is often directed at those we admire, love, or see as examples.

It was important for me to understand this thought as I dealt with verses that speak of sensual or demonically derived wisdom and the turmoil in churches. When God used these harsh, sobering words, He was not speaking to a few twisted, cynical, deliberately wicked, calculating trouble-makers who were out to make the church, the body of Christ, or their homes a "disaster area!" He was speaking to the Patsy's and the me's and the you's who *want* to be purified and desire to see the dross of pride and discord float away, to leave us united in Christ.

After personalizing these thoughts on envy and strife, I realize that the statements in verses 15 through 18 should alert us to honest self-examination. Are we truly drawing on the wisdom from above, or have we subtly slipped back into the world's way of thinking? The presence or absence of envy or strife in our hearts gives us our answer.

Since pride is the root of that uneasiness we feel in the pit of our stomachs when we have reacted to another human being, it shouldn't surprise us to discover the source of such wisdom. James describes it as earthly, sensual and demonic. The world, the flesh, and the devil contribute to an environment full of confusion and every evil work. God wants us to understand that pride will move us away from intimacy with Him and into the world where it is "every man for himself." A holy God cannot have fellowship with sin. Like Gomer we let the downward spiral of pride lead us to our own slave market.

But a ray of light brings hope to our hearts. To show us the contrast between the two kinds of wisdom, James 3:17 provides us with a list of eight qualities of the wisdom from above. This kind of knowledge is first pure then peaceable. It is gentle, reasonable, full of mercy, with good fruit. And, James adds, it is without hypocrisy. This lovely list concludes with an equally beautiful thought: "And the seed whose fruit is righteousness is sown in peace by those who make peace" (James 3:18).

This description of divine wisdom is a vivid picture of the fruit of a righteous person. But, in order to harvest that crop, God must expose and eradicate the weeds that would stifle and choke such a harvest. Weeds like envy, strife, and confusion will blight any harvest.

The closing words of James 3 concern those who make peace, whereas the opening phrases of chapter 4 discuss persons who promote war! Hostility is being described. Although we read in the daily paper about "wars and rumors of wars," these alarms are coming from the local church! Contentions appear and a gruesome battlefield is pictured:

> What is the source of quarrels and conflicts among you? Is not the source your pleasures that wage war in your members? You lust and do not have; so you commit murder. And you are envious and cannot obtain; so you fight and quarrel. You do not have because you do not ask. You ask and do not receive, because you ask with wrong motives, so that you may spend it on your pleasures (James 4:1-3).

Lust, which is desire in any form, is the culprit. Selfishness is a bottomless pit. We remember Pascal's statement concerning knowing Christ personally: "There is a God-shaped vacuum in the heart of every man, which cannot be filled by any created thing, but only by God the creator, made known through Jesus Christ."

In the light of these words, the fighting and desiring described in this assembly of believers must be the result of hearts not fully satisfied in Christ alone. Could it be that they are looking to other people or things to satisfy their longings—which of course, they can't? Isn't there still that gnawing vacuum in any Christian who tries to substitute the sufficiency of Christ with any other thing or person?

These individuals also are pictured as being prayerless. When they do pray, the firm answer is "no," because the request is to satisfy personal desires rather than to seek God's will. Asking amiss is simply masquerading our *wants* as our *needs.*

In the next verse, after discussing the war of pride, James speaks of being adulteresses. Spiritual adultery refers to the perversion of our intimate fellowship and love toward God. The verses surrounding this passage speak of *horizontal relationships* with our fellow man. Jesus connected the two when He was asked which is the *great* commandment in the law:

> ". . . 'You shall love the Lord your God with all your heart, and with all your soul, and with all your mind.' This is the great and foremost commandment. The second is like it, 'You shall love your neighbor as yourself.' On these two commandments depend the whole Law and the Prophets" (Matthew 22:37-40).

When the Lord looks on His bride and sees striving, envying, disputing, and ugliness among those who should be known by their love for each other, He indeed sees spiritual adultery. We cannot be totally abandoned in our love for Him and not love His own. If the lost in the world have not been irresistably drawn to the church to discover the power of God's love, perhaps it is because they are distracted by the battle cries and bloodshed James described.

We could each think of at least one person who has created strife in a local church assembly. Churches have split over the color of carpet to be installed. Someone is always stirring up trouble or complaining. But we can't change those people.

Instead, if *we* would refuse to ever be a party to such a scene again, revival would come! If it did not come to the whole congregation, it would at least come to our individual hearts.

"Ye adulteresses!" This issue will tempt us many times in our Christian life. When we allow things or people to come between us and God, our horizontal relationships will suffer. As John spoke it, we cannot know God without loving:

> Beloved, let us love one another, for love is from God; and everyone who loves is born of God and knows God. The one who does not love does not know God, *for God is love.*

Beloved, if God so loved us, we also ought to love one another (1 John 4:7, 8, 11).

My prayer is that we will be committed to being among the beloved peacemakers. And that every time we begin to strive or "sow discord among the brethren," God will convict us with the piercing sword of His Word:

With it we bless our Lord and Father; and with it we curse men, who have been made in the likeness of God; from the same mouth come both blessing and cursing. My brethren, these things ought not to be this way (James 3:9, 10).

Contention:
It's of the world . . . earthly.
It's of the flesh . . . sensual.
It's of the devil . . . demonical.
The friend of the world is the enemy of God . . .

If we have put the world and its pleasures before God, we have become God's enemy. Ultimately our pride and selfishness will affect our relationships with Him and with others. We will not be peacemakers, but "war" makers—against one another. To avoid Satan's trap, we must examine ourselves. "Adultery?—Pride? *Surely* He is not talking about *me! ---*or *is* He?"

Reflect and Act

Describe your quiet time habits.

What most often robs you of consistent, quality time with God?

If it is coming *before* God, it has made you the *enemy* of God. What do you need to "hold loosely" so that it won't take precedence over your walk with a holy God?

What steps do you need to take to resolve *envy* or *strife* in your heart because of the way you are relating to another person?

What are you counting on to satisfy your heart other than the sufficiency of Christ?

Chapter 13

Humbling
The Proud Heart
James 4:6—5:6

6 But He gives a greater grace. Therefore *it* says, " God is OPPOSED TO THE PROUD, BUT GIVES GRACE TO THE HUM-BLE." 7 Submit therefore to God. Resist the devil and he will flee from you. 8 Draw near to God and He will draw near to you. Cleanse your hands, you sinners; and purify your hearts, you double-minded. 9 Be miserable and mourn and weep; let your laughter be turned into mourning, and your joy to gloom. 10 Humble yourselves in the presence of the Lord, and He will exalt you.

11 Do not speak against one another, brethren. He who speaks against a brother, or judges his brother, speaks against the law, and judges the law; but if you judge the law, you are not a doer of the law, but a judge *of it*. 12 There is *only* one Lawgiver and Judge, the One who is able to save and to destroy; but who are you who judge your neighbor?

13 Come now, you who say, "Today or tomorrow, we shall go to such and such a city, and spend a year there and engage in business and make a profit." 14 Yet you do not know what your life will be like tomorrow. You are *just* a vapor that appears for a little while and then vanishes away. 15 Instead, *you ought* to say, "If the Lord wills, we shall live and also do this or that." 16 But as it is, you boast in your arrogance; all such boasting is evil. 17 Therefore, to one who knows *the* right thing to do, and does not do it, to him it is sin.

Misuse of Riches

5 COME now, you rich, weep and howl for your miseries which are coming upon you. 2 Your riches have rotted and your garments have become moth-eaten. 3 Your gold and your silver have rusted; and their rust will be a witness

against you and will consume your flesh like fire. It is in the last days that you have stored up your treasure! Behold, the pay of the laborers who mowed your fields, *and* which has been withheld by you, cries out *against you;* and the outcry of those who did the harvesting has reached the ears of the Lord of Sabaoth. 5 You have lived luxuriously on the earth and led a life of wanton pleasure; you have fattened your hearts in a day of slaughter. 6 You have condemned and put to death the righteous *man;* he does not resist you.

PERHAPS YOU remember the children's riddle, "Pete and Repeat were sitting on a fence. Pete fell off and who was left? Repeat. Pete and Repeat were sitting on a fence. Pete fell off and . . . ." Once *again* in James we are encouraged to consider:
- —Our attitude toward *God.*
- —Our attitude toward *others.*
- —Our attitude toward *ourselves.*
- —Our attitude toward *riches.*

Since our heavenly Father knows better than anyone that "repetition aids learning," we should appreciate His reminders throughout Scripture. When God feels He needs to repeat basic issues so often, He may want us to see how thick-headed we are and slow to respond to what He has said. A harnessed, humbled heart *should* only have to hear His instruction *once,* and be ready to comply eagerly. But the sad truth is that we quickly forget and often need reminding—like little children.

I once heard the Christian counselor, Dr. Henry Brandt, ask: "How long do we have to ask our children if they remembered to make their beds?" In the silence that followed, the audience anticipated his answer. We knew he had raised his children in a Christian home, instructing them in the Word of God. He was a professional, full-time servant for the Lord. Surely, he had some words of encouragement for this young mother! After eleven years as full-time ministers, having raised our children in a Christian home, I now realize that Dr. Brandt *did* have the answer. In total seriousness, he repeated his question: "*How long* do we have to ask our children if they remembered to make their beds?—T-w-e-n-t-y years!"

One exciting thing about studying Scripture is that in our lifetime we will never plumb the depths of even *one* of His principles, such as, love, forgiveness, humility, the tongue, divine wisdom and power or unity. We will never come to the place where we no longer need *reminding* and further insight. Only the *proud* will say, "Oh, I've learned that—that's not one of my problems." It is *humbling* to consider the loving, creative, *insistent* repetition in God's Word.

The first area where we need renewal is *our attitude toward God*. God desires our humble heart. One reason God resists the proud is that pride causes contention rather than love. We can't *suppress* strife or we'll be poisoned within. An explosion will follow which pollutes the environment around us where love should be thriving. We can't *express* it without finding that our temporary relief from venting hostile feelings only leads to greater harm and makes the mending of strained relationships painfully difficult. If we can't effectively *suppress* or *express* discord, then what are we to do? We must *confess* it, because strife, rooted in pride, is sin.

But exactly *how* are we to overcome the problem and "humble ourselves in the sight of the Lord?" In James 4, verses 7 through 10, the Lord gives clear, precise instruction, if we will take time to think it through. Being meek involves our position toward God, sin and Satan. Perhaps this two-column outline will help us see how we can humble ourselves before God:

ATTITUDE TOWARD THE LORD	ATTITUDE TOWARD SIN AND SATAN
1. Submit to God	2. Resist the devil. (and He will flee from you)
3. Draw near to God (and He will draw near to you).	4. Cleanse your hands (you sinners).
	5. Purify your hearts (you double-minded).
	6. Be miserable and mourn and weep.
	7. Let your laughter be turned into mourning.
	8. Let your joy turn to gloom.

If we do the above, God will perform two things for us: 1) lift us up and 2) give us grace—which is God's perfect provision for our every need. Both James and Peter had thoughts about how we achieve humility. Peter said:

> Clothe yourselves with humility toward one another, God is opposed to the proud, but gives grace to the humble. Humble yourselves, therefore, under the mighty hand of God, that He may exalt you at the proper time, casting all your anxiety upon Him because He cares for you (1 Peter 5:5-7).

The first step in humbling our hearts before the Lord is to submit and the latter part of this passage in 1 Peter tells us *how* to submit. When we cast our cares on God, we *are* submitting to His authority and demonstrating an attitude of trust in His ability to handle our cares adequately. If we *don't* let Him care for us, we are resisting Him with pride. When this occurs, is it any wonder He resists *us?*

The person we are to resist is the devil and this is the second step in renewing our attitude toward God. Submitting to God and resisting the devil should be inseparable. When we yield to God by laying our concern upon Him in prayer, and trusting Him with our lives, you can be *sure* the enemy will be in hot pursuit to defeat us! He hates to see active allegiance to God!

Satan is real, and he is our enemy. He is subtle, and many in the church are slow to identify his work and deal with him scripturally. We need to know our enemy! Otherwise, we will fail to fight for the victories that are ours for the taking. If we are Christian soldiers (and 2 Timothy says we are), the battle is not against flesh and blood, but with principalities, powers and the rulers of darkness. There *is* an enemy and a war — there are battles to be fought and won. If we are swinging blindly at the air or taking pot shots at each other in frustration, the enemy stands by enjoying an easy victory. It must look comical to him to see an army of soldiers fighting *each other* and swinging wildly as we curse his presence.

After Peter tells us *how* to submit to God, he states *why* this is important and *how* to resist the devil: "Be of sober spirit, be on the alert. Your adversary, the devil, prowls about like a roaring lion, seeking someone to devour. But resist him, firm in your faith . . . " (1 Peter 5:8, 9).

In order to be sober, vigilant and steadfast in faith, we must dress ourselves in the spiritual armor of Ephesians 6. To withstand supernatural evil forces, we must have our loins girded with truth, wear a breastplate of righteousness, have our feet shod with the preparation of the gospel of peace, hold the shield of faith, wear the helmet of salvation, and wield the sword of the Spirit which is God's Word. And we must stand, dressed in this unseen armor, in constant prayer!

We can imagine a scriptural "knight in shining armor!" But do we *really* see ourselves *daily* relying on each of these provisions to keep us secure from the evil lion, who wants to render us useless for the service of God?

When have we last claimed *the blood of the Lamb* as our cloak of righteousness? Satan's forces *know* that Christ's shed blood defeats them! When recently have we resisted the devil by claiming the authority of *Jesus' name* according to Philippians 2:9, 10? When have we confessed Scripture to dispel Satan's attack? Jesus quoted Scripture when He was tempted in the wilderness. He knew it was the offensive weapon given to fight the enemy. Hebrews 4:12 reveals that God's Word is *sharper* than a two-edged sword. Do we *know* and *use* our offensive weapon to secure spiritual victories?

If we are attempting to submit to God and walk with Jesus, we *are* encountering spiritual warfare! The question is, are we *identifying* spiritual, unseen warfare for what it is? Satan and all of the demons did not just disappear when Jesus ascended to heaven. We need to know our enemy! If we will remember the three-pronged weapon — the *blood* of Jesus, the *name* of Jesus, and the *Word* of Jesus, we will be more prepared for our enemy. A Christian soldier needs to know and *fight* his enemy in the power of the Holy Spirit, utilizing the whole armor of God.

The third step in humbling ourselves is to *draw near* to God. It is one thing to cast our burdens and cares at His feet. It is another to draw near to Him. Many of us are looking for a place to dump our cares! But are we willing to linger and experience the *presence* of the Burden-Bearer? The command is for us to *draw near* — not to say, "Give me a sense of Your presence and I'll join You." His desire is for us to take the initiative with a childlike expectancy and seek His presence. This takes time, diligence and discipline. However, when we come eagerly to Jesus, our lives are renewed, refreshed and overflowing.

Steps four and five reveal why it is humbling to draw near to god. In His presence we are stripped of pretense and become aware of our need to "cleanse our hands" — confess *external* activities that displease Him — and "purify our hearts" — confess *internal* activities that offend Him. His light reveals the darkness in us, and to deal with it is both humbling and uplifting.

The sixth point of instruction is to be afflicted and to mourn and weep. As step seven and eight continue, our laughter is to be turned into mourning and our joy to gloom. What is God saying to us? Is He saying that He wants our Christian experience to be miserable and unbearable? Could it be that the silly rumor Satan spread about the Christian life being "straight-laced, sober and sad" is true? Of course not! Jesus came "that we might have life and have it *abundantly*" (John 10:10). Then, what *is* God saying?

We are reading these words to discover how to humble ourselves in the sight of the Lord. We will never be humble if we are standing erect (God calls it "stiff-necked") and justifying any behavior that is less than holy. When is the last time we have grieved, wept, mourned and felt actual pain and heaviness from the weight of a sin in our life? It's easy to get upset over the sins of another—but what about our own sin? We will *never* conquer a sin over which we do not *grieve*. We must hate what God hates! We must see sin as He sees it. It cost Him much to provide us with forgiveness. How can we giggle over it, condone it or pamper it?

Recently I was devastated when God convicted me of a sin that I had been tolerating. It was bedtime and lights were out. My heart was so heavy I thought it would break. It was too painful to lie there suppressing tears, so I slipped out of bed and went down to the living room with my Bible. I know 1 John 1:9 and believe in thorough cleansing and forgiveness for the asking. But this particular night, it was not that simple. I sobbed, grieved and experienced *mourning*. Once I verbalized these emotions to God, I pored over the Beatitudes:

> "Blessed are the poor in spirit, for theirs is the kingdom
> of heaven. Blessed are those who mourn, for they shall be
> comforted" (Matthew 5:3, 4).

Once again I was thankful for the scribbled notes along the margin of my Bible. Eagerly, I read the brief thoughts: "We experience God's comfort when we experience grief. Mourning is sorrow that begins in the heart—but it takes over the whole person. This sorrow is over spiritual failure or actual sin. It is a sense of spiritual poverty—an awareness of unlikeness to Christ which brings regret and contrition—but is *not incompatible with rejoicing!"*

The *joy* of the Lord was restored as I realized the humility I was experiencing as I took the sin that had afflicted me and grieved, with the Holy Spirit, over the crippling effect it would have if not dealt with.

As we consider *our attitude toward God and our need for renewal,* we must believe His desire is to lift us up and give us His grace. But He will not do this for the proud heart. First we must "humble ourselves in His sight.

The second area where the Christian needs renewal is in *our attitude toward others.* James 4 began with a sad commentary on church relationships. The first two verses described something akin to a battlefield: wars, fightings, lust and killing — hardly an atmosphere conducive to worship and drawing near to God!

After we have been advised to deal with pride and humble ourselves before God, we are confronted with our need for renewal in human relationships:

> Do not speak against one another, brethren. He who speaks against a brother, or judges his brother, speaks against the law, and judges the law; but if you judge the law, you are not a doer of the law, but a judge of it.
>
> There is only one Lawgiver and Judge, the One who is able to save and to destroy; but who are you who judge your neighbor? (James 4:11, 12)

A paraphrase of this passage might be helpful. If we speak evil of another person, in essence we are judging that the law of love is wrong. Somehow we reason that because we are able to see what is wrong with others, we should therefore have the freedom to discuss it! God calls it pride. Our pride, *not* discernment, causes us to judge others by *our* standard. When they fall short, we make them feel or sound "small" in the eyes of others.

God is the only lawgiver and the only one that is to judge. Our concern should be to discern so we can pray and *encourage* each other toward the mark of His high calling. Renewal would come if we would only exhort, rebuke, encourage, challenge and keep His great commandment — "Owe nothing to anyone except to love one another; for he that loves his neighbor has fulfilled the law" (Romans 13:8). Our concern should be to *fulfill* the law, not to *judge* it.

The next time we are tempted to speak evil about a fellow believer, we must stop to think about his worth. The worth of any object is its purchase price—and that brother or sister in Christ was purchased with the blood of Jesus. Before judging, we should imagine taking that person with us to the foot of the cross. As we stand there to tell Jesus the wrong we see, we should think of the purchase price He paid for *both* of us. We must meditate on Christ's love for this person until we know it has humbled our arrogant, superior spirit. If we stand beneath the cross of Jesus long enough, the lawgiver will soften our hearts with His love. He may have to break them, but He will *renew* our attitude and eventually our relationship with others. How can we speak evil of someone God was willing to redeem with His beloved Son's life? It's impossible—if we're willing to check our attitude toward others, confess pride where it exists and admit the need for renewal.

Equally important as our relationship with others is the third area, *our attitudes about ourselves*. James stresses that we should not think more highly of ourselves than is necessary for a healthy sense of self worth.

> Come now, you who say, "Today or tomorrow, we shall go to such and such a city, and spend a year there and engage in business and make a profit." Yet you do not know what your life will be like tomorrow. You are just a vapor that appears for a little while and then vanishes away. Instead, you ought to say, "If the Lord wills, we shall live and also do this or that." But as it is, you boast in your arrogance; all such boasting is evil. Therefore, to one who knows the right thing to do, and does not do it, to him it is sin (James 4:13-17).

But we are presumptuous! Our *pride* and selfish ambition materialize in our subtle insistence to "run the show." Somehow we think that if we are forceful enough, we will see things go our way. We may—but once again, we will be blazing that trail alone!

In this passage, James describes these Christians as *assuming* their ability to succeed by *boasting* of four things:
- Their goal.
- How they will achieve it.
- When they will do it.
- How long they will do it.

This is a classic description of a person who seriously believes he is "the captain of his ship and the master of his fate." We would expect this confidence in one's own resources from "a worldling." Unbelievers have no other resource! But this is a warning to those who believe in drawing near to God.

On the other hand, "if we aim at nothing we will hit it *every* time." We *are* to set goals rather than drifting in a vacuum. We *are* to make plans to move forward rather than standing still. But we cannot lose sight of our total dependence on God. He is Lord of life and Lord of all, even our well-laid plans. We will begin to discover His will and His leading when we inject a new phrase into our praying and planning processes: not "I will, I will, I will," like Satan when he fell; but "if the Lord wills" — the attitude of dependence.

We saw a beautiful example of planning and moving out, balanced with dependence and seeking the Father's wisdom when our son was only 11 and took a paper route. David was determined to do it himself. He wanted to grow up and be independent. His attitude was almost cocky as he reviewed with us: *what* he was going to do, how it would take place, when it was going to happen and for how long. "No sweat," as the kids would say! But the night before his first run, he was not quite so sure of himself. He knew it would be dark when he left the house at 5:30 a.m., and he was frightened.

Dave and I had been out for the evening, so the kids were in bed when we came in. But David's light was on in his bedroom. When we peeked in, he asked us if we would pray for him, and through his prayers we became aware of his apprehension. By sheer inspiration, Daddy asked, "Son, how 'bout if I go with you the first morning just to make sure you can see all the house numbers? We'll make that run together, and then you'll be on your own."

David thought that was a super idea. As we started to cross the hall to our bedroom, he said, "You know, I don't know what I was so frightened about. I'm not afraid any more at all!" The unknown is not so scary when we know our Father is with us.

After that first morning, David took off on his own in the dark. I would lie in bed, listening for the garage door to roll open. Out would come his bike with the flashlight, and off he would sail with his Snoopy hat pulled down over his ears, to deliver those sixty-plus papers. I wanted to go and shield him from racoons, possums, dogs, snow, rain and traffic — the unknown. But he needed to learn "independent-dependence" on us and on the

Lord.

Each morning as I heard David leave, I prayed that God would use this route to build character into his life — like when King David was in "sheep school" preparing to serve God. We don't have sheep around here, but we do have daily papers! And David has delivered them for several years. There have been times he has come to the edge of the bed, dripping wet, when the lightning was heavy — and we have finished the route with him. Other times he has asked us for prayer. But through it all, he has learned to be less presumptuous and more dependent on His heavenly Father.

Some individuals cannot cope easily with dependence upon another. I remember talking with a woman about where she stood with God. She told me *no one* was going to order her around! "Why," she exclaimed, "I plan to die when I am good and ready — and not before!" Can you imagine this intelligent, educated woman really believing and boasting that she alone was the lord of her life? That is the extreme. But sometimes Christian attitudes seem almost as insulting when it comes to the goals and routines of life. They seem to say, "Stick around, God, and save me when it's time to leave this world, but I've got plans and I need breathing room. So for now, keep Your hands off the steering wheel while You occupy *this* vehicle!"

Maybe we should meditate more often on the brevity of life as James pointed out in verse 14: "Yet you do not know what your life will be like tomorrow. You are just a vapor that appears for a little while and then vanishes away." Do you like being called a vapor? It's quite a contrast to the self-sufficient, self-controlled philosophy of the world that tries to convince us that we are indestructible. To admit to being a vapor is humbling! To pretend we are invincible is presumptuous. We must analyze our attitudes about ourselves and our approach to planning and implementing the goals we've set for our lives. They may need renewing.

The fourth area we may need to examine is *our attitude toward riches*. James was not lenient in his admonitions toward the rich:

> Come now, you rich, weep and howl for your miseries which are coming upon you. Your riches have rotted and your garments have become moth-eaten. Your gold and your silver have rusted; and their rust will be a witness against

you and will consume your flesh like fire. It is in the last days that you have stored up your treasure!

Behold, the pay of the laborers who mowed your fields, and which has been withheld by you, cries out against you; and the outcry of those who did the harvesting has reached the ears of the Lord of Sabaoth. You have lived luxuriously on the earth and led a life of wanton pleasure; you have fattened your hearts in a day of slaughter. You have condemned and put to death the righteous man; he does not resist you (James 5:1-6).

God is interested in our stewardship of all He has entrusted to us. In this area the rich can be sabotaged by self-indulgence to the extreme of mistreating others.

Improperly invested wealth, hoarding rather than giving, unsacrificial giving, and withholding fair payment to those who have labored are common worldly misuses of money. But the church is supposed to be different!

The world is upside down! They have riches first, themselves second, others third and God out there somewhere. God's Word is trying to turn us right side up: God first, then caring for others, and finally a proper perspective about our own planning and riches. A paraphrase of Romans 12:2 might read: "Stop being conformed to this world! Quit letting it squeeze you into its mold! You can be renewed and transformed if you will synchronize your attitudes with God's plans for worshiping, relating to others, and investing your life and riches for His glory!"

Whether this happens in the lives of individual Christians will depend upon if we grasp *the essence of stewardship.* It is declared in Romans 11:36: "For from Him and through Him and *to* Him are all things. To Him be the glory forever." Everything is His. An owner has rights, but a steward has responsibilities. If we own anything we have taken it from God. We will never become free in our giving if we think ourselves the owners of what we have and give. The one who "heaps up treasure for himself" does not take seriously the stewardship entrusted to him when he became a child of the King and owner of all.

I'm convinced that healthy Christians give freely. They drink from Jesus and out of them *flows* generosity. There is no holding back, no greed, no restraints, no insensitivity. The humble soul will draw near to God, drink from His resources, and eagerly pour out money and good works. He doesn't wonder who is trying to take advantage of him or who is giving more or less. He only wants to do all he can to contribute to a healthy, vital, prosperous, fruitful church.

Giving generously is directly associated with the filling of the Holy Spirit. Nothing will have to be squeezed out of us, if we are allowing Him the freedom to fill us and flow from us. Are we hoarding or giving? Are we concentrating on God's work or our pleasure? When the Spirit-filled life is *taught* from the pulpits and *applied* from the pews, we need not worry about *self-indulgence.* The Spirit-filled heart is renewed and generously flows!

As I look at the lack of joy and of Christ's pre-eminence in the church, I'm convinced that God is calling for *renewal.* Not occasionally, when we get dried up and need a "spiritual shot in the arm" — but daily through His Word. *Renewal* does not mean a passive existence that waits on God to shake us up, but it denotes a life of action. Observe the numerous *action* words used in James 4 and 5: submit, resist, draw near, cleanse, purify, be, let, humble yourself, weep and howl.

There is no recipe here for instant sanctification or quick victory. Some of our pride patterns are ingrained deeply. Below the surface is the spirit of independence and the cloaked deification of self! We cannot rapidly identify and recoil from the subtle, obscure undercurrents of pride. But our Lord and Master is keenly interested in our eradicating egotism in *any* form.

In Proverbs 6:17-19, Solomon records seven things that God hates, which are dealt with in James' epistle to the church:

— haughty eyes;
— a lying tongue;
— hands that shed innocent blood;
— a heart that devises wicked plans;
— feet that run rapidly to evil;
— a false witness who utters lies;
— one who spreads strife among brothers.

As God pinpointed these areas, the believer was covered from top to bottom: eyes, tongue, hands, heart and feet. Three of the items listed relate to our tongues, and pride leads the pack!

The Word teaches in Psalm 51:17:

> "The sacrifices of God are a broken spirit;
> A broken and a contrite heart, O God, thou wilt not despise."

Will we let our hearts be broken over the sins that God hates?

If we ask God to reveal pride and if we will humble ourselves, He is waiting to lift us up. He wants to draw near to us, not push us away. But He requires a humble heart and our initiating action to do so. Clearly, Christians, it's our move!

Reflect and Act

Here is your opportunity to personalize the four-point outline:

1. MY attitude toward *God* . . . and the need for renewal:

2. MY attitude toward *others* . . . and the need for renewal:

3. MY attitude toward *myself* . . . and the need for renewal:

4. MY attitude toward *riches* (and giving) . . . and the need for renewal:

Chapter 14

Focus On Fine Tuning
James 5:7-20

7 Be patient, therefore, brethren, until the coming of the Lord. Behold, the farmer waits for the precious produce of the soil, being patient about it, until it gets the early and late rains. 8 You too be patient; strengthen your hearts, for the coming of the Lord is at hand. 9 Do not complain, brethren, against one another, that you yourselves may not be judged; behold, the Judge is standing right at the door. 10 As an example, brethren, of suffering and patience, take the prophets who spoke in the name of the Lord. 11 Behold, we count those blessed who endured. You have heard of the endurance of Job and have seen the outcome of the Lord's dealings, that the Lord is full of compassion and *is* merciful.

12 But above all, my brethren, do not swear, either by heaven or by earth or with any other oath; but let your yes be yes, and you no, no; so that you may not fall under judgment.

13 Is anyone among you suffering? Let him pray. Is anyone cheerful? Let him sing praises. 14 Is anyone among you sick? Let him call for the elders of the church, and let them pray over him, anointing him with oil in the name of the Lord; 15 and the prayer offered in faith will restore the one who is sick, and the Lord will raise him up, and if he has committed sins, they will be forgiven him. 16 Therefore, confess your sins to one another, and pray for one another, so that you may be healed. The effective prayer of a righteous man can accomplish much. 17 Elijah was a man with a nature like ours, and he prayed earnestly that it might not rain; and it did not rain on the earth for three years and six months. 18 And he prayed again, and the sky poured rain, and the earth produced its fruit.

19 My brethren, if any among you strays from the truth, and one turns him back, 20 let him know that he who turns

a sinner from the error of his way will save his soul from death, and will cover a multitude of sins.

WHEN HER class in the book of 1 Thessalonians was dismissed, Jeanne made a beeline for home. She had never been in a Bible study before, and was amazed at what she had been told in the lecture that day!

"Gunnar!" she called, as she dashed through the front of the house, looking for him along the way.

She found him sitting on the edge of the tub, caulking the tile. "Gunnar, have you *heard?*" she asked excitedly.

"Have I heard *what?*"

"That Jesus Christ is coming *again*?"

"Well, yes, I think I've heard that before."

"Well, why didn't someone tell *me?*"

There they sat, perched precariously on bathroom fixtures, discussing the most exciting event yet to take place in the history of planet earth — and it was news to Jeanne! The awesome scope of God's eternal plan soon led Jeanne to a personal relationship with Jesus Christ. After having seen Him in the context of all history, she was ready to forsake all and follow her Maker and Master.

The subject of the return of Christ is *not* isolated to the book of Revelation, as I once thought. It is injected as a note of encouragement throughout the entire Bible. To look at life in light of eternity helps us not to be entangled with trivia, but committed to essentials. Life takes on proper perspective when we are *focused* on Jesus Christ and the "big picture."

It *should* fill our hearts with hope and expectancy when we run across the many verses declaring His return:

". . . and they will see the Son of Man coming on the clouds of the sky with power and great glory" (Matthew 24:30).

"Men of Galilee, why do you stand looking into the sky? This Jesus, who has been taken up from you into heaven, will come in just the same way as you have watched Him go into heaven" (Acts 1:11).

For our citizenship is in heaven, from which also we eagerly wait for a Savior, the Lord Jesus Christ (Philippians 3:20).

For the Lord Himself will descend from heaven with a shout, with the voice of the archangel, and with the trumpet of God; and the dead in Christ shall rise first. Then we who are alive and remain shall be caught up together with them in the clouds to meet the Lord in the air, and thus we shall always be with the Lord. Therefore comfort one another with these words (1 Thessalonians 4:16-18).

God wants us to be *comforted by the prospect of His return.* Though there are trials and afflictions to be faced, the battle has already been won. There *is* victory in Jesus!

In this book we have looked at many Scriptures, particularly in James, which closely examine many areas of "the flesh" that must be yielded to the Spirit's control if we are to be godly people. The exhortations have come rapidly, like "rabbit punches." We are clearly told, "In the world you have tribulation, but take courage; I have overcome the world" (John 16:33). The Bible actually ends on this note of expectancy about the Lord's return: "He who testifies to these things says, 'Yes, I am coming quickly.' Amen. Come, Lord Jesus" (Revelation 22:20). The book of James also ends with this hope. While he offers three more exhortations concerning patience, praying and confronting one another, he says it in light of Christ's coming.

James' concern for his brethren is touching. His constant stress on practical, vital Christian living has not been to batter and bruise us into defeat — but to challenge and motivate us and direct us to paths of joy and victory, regardless of our circumstances. He has made bold statements to alert us to God's fine-tuning so we will be comfortable and unashamed when we one day meet our Lord.

James spoke of patience in chapter one and prayer in chapter four but has spent the *entire letter* demonstrating his desire to see Christians assume the responsibility to rebuke the sinner from error. In his closing paragraph he re-emphasizes the importance of these three things by summarizing them before a panoramic backdrop of the Lord's return.

Be patient, therefore, brethren, until the coming of the Lord. Behold, the farmer waits for the precious produce of the soil, being patient about it, until it gets the early and late rains. You too be patient; strengthen your hearts, for the coming of the Lord is at hand. Do not complain, brethren, against one another, that you yourselves may not be judged; behold, the Judge is standing right at the door. As an example, brethren, of suffering and patience, take the prophets who spoke in the name of the Lord. Behold, we count those blessed who endured. You have heard of the endurance of Job and have seen the outcome of the Lord's dealings, that the Lord is full of compassion and is merciful.

But above all, my brethren, do not swear, either by heaven or by earth or with any other oath; but let your yes be yes, and your no, no; so that you may not fall under judgment (James 5:7-12).

We are encouraged by James to be patient like the farmer, not irritated and anxious over things we can't control or change. We are admonished to be persistent, weeding discouragement from a cultivated, established heart, trusting God for growth. We steadily develop diligence with others, not holding grudges, and we strive to be "response-able," not judgmental. From the prophets example we cultivate long-suffering. And from Job's dilemma, we learn to practice perseverance, and thereby subjugate deep suffering. "And the Lord restored the fortunes of Job when he prayed for his friends, and the Lord increased all that Job had twofold" (Job 42:10). And in all situations, we can remain submissive rather than defensive, answering *yes* or *no*.

One example after another is used to make the same point — *be patient!* When God goes to the trouble to say the same thing so many different ways, we can be sure He wants us to understand that His point is both imperative and significant.

We can impatiently focus on the weather, our fruitfulness, our circumstances, our hearts, others or "making our point." *Or* we can deal with each of these areas while patiently *focusing* on the Lord. The choice is ours.

Yet we so often are tempted to succumb to impatience! We like to see things happen — be involved in motion and progress. And when circumstances or people put us in a "hold pattern," we balk! We want our labor to bear fruit *now*. We desire people to change immediately. Why else would we murmur against them? We covet deliverance at once from affliction. Who wishes to endure like Job — patient *until the coming of the Lord?* Sure — if He would come presently, but He has taken two thousand years already! We say, *now*. He says *patiently* "– – – Occupy till I come" (Luke 19:13 KJV). We will be patient to the degree we trust in His timing in our lives and the unrolling of His eternal plan.

One summer I was at a standstill in several areas of ministry. We were pursuing many ideas, but *nothing* was falling into place. We ran into one brick wall after another. I called it "pivoting in place with one foot nailed down!" While I prayed, "Thy will be done," it seemed as though *nothing* was being achieved.

I tried to be patient, but I often failed. The Lord held me still until *He* was ready to move and then He allowed the days that followed to be among the most fruitful in my journey with Him. We cannot *make* something happen in the spiritual walk. If He's in the objective, it will happen in *His* time. If He's not, we wouldn't want it anyway.

As James moves from the subject of patience to prayer, it is easy to connect the two. How better to practice patience than to pray? It is in prayer that we come boldly to the throne of grace to obtain mercy in time of need. We humbly cast our cares upon the Lord and wait patiently for His provision. In prayer we *focus* on the Lord, adoring, worshipping and praising Him with thankful hearts. James placed a high priority on prayer:

> Is anyone among you suffering? Let him pray. Is anyone cheerful? Let him sing praises. Is anyone among you sick? Let him call for the elders of the church, and let them pray over him, anointing him with oil in the name of the Lord; and the prayer offered in faith will restore the one who is sick, and the Lord will raise him up, and if he has committed sins, they will be forgiven him. Therefore, confess your sins to one another, and pray for one another, so that you may be healed. The effective prayer of a righteous man can accomplish much (James 5:13-16).

Daily life is composed of both afflictions and blessings. We will be praying *without ceasing* as commanded in I Thessalonians 5:17, if we are praying over both troubles and joys.

As the ordained leaders of the church are called to the bedside of those who are ill, spiritual authority is being demonstrated. Some of our friends, who called for the elders once in a time of illness, have assured us that it was a very special time of knowing the Lord's presence.

As we pray, we are instructed to confess our faults horizontally, as well as vertically. If we obeyed this instruction, there would be an incredible amount of physical, emotional and spiritual healing taking place. We are eager to "share" our problems, but not our faults. There *is* a big difference! Pride, once again, holds us back.

The prayer of faith focuses on His able power and perfect will at work on our behalf. We were warned not to be presumptuous in planning, but to say, "if it be thy will." And when Jesus instructed us, He told us to pray, "Thy will be done, on earth as it is in heaven." James explains that when our prayers are answered "No," it is because we pray amiss — simply wanting our own way more than His will.

During the summer when I found myself not moving in ministry, I clung to a Scripture verse.

> I would have despaired unless I had believed that I would
> see the goodness of the Lord
> In the land of the living.
> Wait for the Lord;
> Be strong and let your heart take courage;
> Yes, wait for the Lord (Psalms 27:13,14).

As it was beautifully full of hope and promise, I claimed this verse concerning *one* thing I was praying for in faith.

The summer dragged on and that verse stayed over my kitchen sink. I kept waiting patiently, fully expecting to see God's goodness. But the response to every lead we had was *no*. After fervent prayer, expectant prayer, ceaseless prayer and corporate prayer, the answer was still *no*.

As I prepared to teach the book of Luke in the fall, I paused to meditate on the ask, seek, knock passage in chapter 11. How, I wondered, could we be so involved in all three prayer actions and still be receiving no for an answer? My assistant Janee was the one to share a simple statement that helped break the pivoting cycle. She said, "He loves us *so* much. He will only do what is *best* for us. You sincerely think you've been asking for an egg — but He must know it's a scorpion!" Janee lovingly helped me understand that I *had* seen the goodness of the Lord — not in the granting of my request, but in protection from "scorpions."

As I look back on that troublesome ordeal, patience, prayer and rebuking in love were all involved. It took awhile, but my eyes again focused on the Giver, instead of the gift. That special prayer may yet be answered — but it will be in His time, not mine! Earnest prayer doesn't always assure that the answer will be to our liking, but it *will* be for our benefit.

In verses 17 and 18, James reminds us of Elijah who prayed the prayer of faith with remarkable results.

> Elijah was a man with a nature like ours, and he prayed
> earnestly that it might not rain; and it did not rain on the

earth for three years and six months. And he prayed again, and the sky poured rain, and the earth produced its fruit (James 5:17, 18).

He was given a unique opportunity to glorify God mightily, but it is interesting to note that Elijah went from believing, persevering prayer to utter defeat. He let some upsetting news cause fear.

Then Jezebel sent a messenger to Elijah, saying, "So may the gods do to me and even more, if I do not make your life as the life of one of them by tomorrow about this time." And he was afraid and arose and ran for his life and came to Beersheba, which belongs to Judah, and left his servant there (1 Kings 19:2, 3).

After the victory comes the "roaring lion seeking whom he may devour." Elijah was a pooped prophet who let disappointment and depression wipe him out completely.

He fled, sulked, and resisted warnings, until God removed him from further service. God rebuked him twice in an attempt to restore him and release him from fear. ". . . and behold, the word of the Lord came to him, and He said to him, 'What are you doing here, Elijah?" (1 Kings 19:9) God was executing what James instructs us to do in the last two verses of chapter 5 — care enough to exhort the erring and rebuke the rebellious. In like manner, we are encouraged to help correct the one who is straying from the truth:

My brethren, if any among you strays from the truth, and one turns him back, let him know that he who turns a sinner from the error of his way will save his soul from death, and will cover a multitude of sins (James 5:19, 20).

We shudder to fulfill this commandment because to do so means risking rejection. But the command to love and our desire to see Christ glorified encourage us to assume the responsibility of these last two verses. James wrote an entire epistle exhorting those that err. His purpose was for our good. He hoped to shed light on our "blind spots" and cause us to "walk in the light as He Himself is in the light . . . [having] fellowship with one another" (1 John 1:7). There is no fellowship in darkness, because our focus and perspective are obliterated!

When a doctor sees a dark spot on an x-ray, he does not hide the fact from the patient for fear of upsetting him or hurting his feelings. He gently explains the problems and takes steps to have the spot removed — *knowing* pain and healing will be involved! We cannot *make* our brother face surgery, but we *can* help him identify the black spot that needs removal by the Great Physician. Jesus warned Peter that he would deny Him and then assured him he would be converted. He was already a believer, but he would have to get "turned around" to know Christ's victory. Otherwise he would walk in *death*. "For the mind set on the flesh is death, but the mind set on the Spirit is life and peace" (Romans 8:6). There is no one more miserable than the carnal Christian who has at one time tasted "life and peace." He's like a walking corpse — alive, but dead when it comes to spiritual vitality.

Not everyone who is confronted with their error will respond with a teachable, grateful spirit. But at least they can never say, *"Why* didn't you care enough to help me see the error of my ways?" The affects of our attempts are not always realized with the first reaction. We may see repentance, restoration and growth far down the road — in *His* time.

The Bible gives us quite a few nudges concerning this business of rebuking, and we are encouraged to consider several things when we are *called* to this unpleasant, easy-to-be avoided ministry. Therefore, a few guidelines will help facilitate what the Word commands us to do.

First, church discipline begins when one offended party rebukes another. Since it is seldom practiced, we reap the results of moral decay.

"And if your brother sins, go and reprove him in private; if he listens to you, you have won your brother" (Matthew 18:15).

This procedure usually breaks down when the offended party focuses on the offense and talks to *others* about the complaint. The offended person fains friendship, but harbors a grudge. A grudge is simply a relationship interrupted by an offense which has festered and not been dealt with.

Better is open rebuke
Than love that is concealed.
Faithful are the wounds of a friend,
But deceitful are the kisses of an enemy (Proverbs 27:5, 6).

Secondly, when we fail to rebuke, we are withdrawing from spiritual battle and handing the enemy a victory without so much as a skirmish. Shouldn't we make an *attempt* to help one get back in fellowship with the Lord? Wouldn't that demonstrate true love and friendship more than our silence?

> And the Lord's bond-servant must not be quarrelsome, but be kind to all, able to teach, patient when wronged, with gentleness correcting those who are in opposition, if perhaps God may grant them repentance leading to the knowledge of the truth, and they may come to their senses and escape from the snare of the devil, having been held captive by him to do his will (2 Timothy 2:24-26).

Finally, if we are not filled with the Holy Spirit when we rebuke others, they will not sense His Spirit "speaking the truth in love." Instead they will sense the mood of strife, which is not from above. ". . . For since there is jealousy and strife among you, are you not fleshly . . . ?" (1 Corinthians 3:3). It is hard to believe that a rebuke is being given in our best interest, if the "deliverer" is up tight and out of control. The person admonishing appears to be striking out and inflicting pain rather than bringing healing and sanctification. And our natural response is to "take cover!"

Spiritual rebuke is an act of love—and others will know when it's done in that disposition. So, we need to take time to be sure that our motives are right, our understanding clear, and our hearts pure.

> Brethren, even if a man is caught in any trespass, you who are spiritual, restore such a one in a spirit of gentleness; each one looking to yourself, lest you too be tempted (Galatians 6:1).

In Matthew 7 Jesus encouraged us to help the brother with the speck in his eye. We *need* help with our flaws. But He warned us to first handle our own "logs"—our attitudes about our brother's faults. If we don't deal with our motives first, it will be the blind leading the blind, swinging wildly at one another's shortcomings. Somebody is bound to get hurt when this occurs.

Dave and I have dedicated our lives to the Great Commission—"Go and make disciples!" We believe that command is to be taken seriously, and we have begun at home with our two children. Part of the nurturing or discipling process is to rebuke and restore. As we assume the responsibility to build lives, there is no way to avoid growing pains and the need for instruction and correction. It is easier if the person is teachable. But when someone is caught in a fault, we can't count on that.

It was a thrill when Katie and I were first asked to speak at a Mother-Daughter banquet. The Lord was at work in Katie's life, and she was blossoming into a lovely young Christian teen. We were both eager to represent Christ together!

But a week before the event, she and her dad started getting "sideways" with one another. They are so much alike in character that they easily "lock horns" if the Lord is not in charge. It is usually those most like us that irritate us the most. We don't like to look in the mirror because we see what the Lord hasn't yet transformed. For several mornings Katie gave her dad a hard time. She would huff and puff, and finally storm off to school, leaving the house full of tension and gloom.

Before handling the problem with Katie, I first had to work through the striving in my own heart, because I resented the interruption in our peaceful home. Regaining my perspective on His sovereign control, I was able to walk through the rebuking process demonstrating patience, prayer and care.

Dave didn't know that I called Katie at school and arranged to pick her up. We drove to a side street where I quietly reviewed her recent behavior. I gave her some scriptural principles I felt she was violating, let her share her side, had prayer, and took her home. The one thing I made sure she understood, was that we would *not* publically speak of Christ's love, and be hypocrites!

It was hard to tell how she had received my rebuke as we drove home in icy silence. Slamming the car door, she ran inside the house and up the stairs. My heart sank. The discipline had been given with love. Now, all I could do was be patient and pray.

Later that evening, Dave came down the stairs. His eyes were misty and his face beaming. Never asking what had transpired he took me in his arms and whispered, "I don't know what you did, but thanks."

Blessed *are* the peacemakers! Rebuking is not fun or easy but it *is* an act of love. And when you see one restored to fellowship with God and others, it is sweet compensation. If it were only as easy to deal with Christian brothers and sisters as it is with our children! We will persevere, if we really care. As we do, our prayer has to be: "God, deliver us from being unduly critical! But free us also from "cotton-candy Christianity" where we refuse to become deeply involved in relationships — where we do *anything* to avoid an unpleasant confrontation!"

This is a tediously painful principle for most of us to apply. Our society has taught us to retreat behind fences, doors and masks. We've learned not to risk vulnerability by taking chances in relating. The walls meant to protect others from getting in often become prisons that keep us from getting out.

As we evaluate the danger, we might consider these questions. Do we want to see our friends become more like the Savior? Do *we* desire to reflect a greater amount of His image — enough to let others correct us? Do we resist friendships where, "Iron sharpens iron, so one man sharpens another" (Proverbs 27:17)? Iron scraping against iron can be an unnerving thing. Can we love and accept the people God sends as "sandpaper" into our lives? Once when I asked a lady that question, she rolled her eyes and groaned. Is our response toleration, instead of loving acceptance?

I'm asking these questions because we cannot "dish it out" in love if we haven't learned to "take it" the same way. It's a two way street, with much at stake. If we consider both sides we can save one another from carnally minded death!

A dead person cannot see. And neither can a person who is walking in darkness. "If we say that we have fellowship with Him and yet walk in the darkness, we lie and do not practice the truth" (1 John 1:6). The truth is full of light, but we cannot see it or apply it if we are walking in death and darkness. God's plan is to use His servants to lead stumbling brothers back to the path of joy. The carnally-minded Christian who needs to be rebuked, exhorted and counseled concerning sin also has misplaced discernment as he wanders in darkness and death. If he cannot *discern* truth from error, his decisions will perpetuate the downward spiral.

God recently changed my views on how to receive discernment. I have often seen a lack of perception in Christians who intersperse Bible teachings with philosophies of the world. They receive a little truth and then make some off-the-wall statement — in light of what "Scripture" teaches! This approach is deadly! I have always prayed for God to give such people discernment. I have also advised others to pray for their own insight. It was only recently that Scripture revealed the error of my approach. Psalms 111:10 has changed my prayer and counsel:

> The fear of the Lord is the beginning of wisdom;
> A good understanding have all those who do His command-
> ments.

I need not pray for a friend to be given discernment, if he will not do or obey what he knows of God's truth! Instead, I must pray for him to be willing to apply Christ's commandments as I remind him what they are. Then God will grant him intelligence to know how.

Reflect and Act

Join with me in this final exercise of taking what God has said in His Word and *applying* it to our individual lives.

In light of the Lord's coming, and ALL of eternity, I'm willing to:

be patient about God's timing in:

pray, in faith, about:

risk rejection by rebuking in love if it will help:

apply what I am learning and go and make disciples because:

As we reflect on what James has set before us, I appreciate God's unrelenting persistence to stir us up and spark our desire to live holy, Christ-centered lives. It will cost us *everything* of self to know the fulness of His joy. In our trial-troubled times, we will need to be reminded of these "basics" when the road gets rocky, and we're tempted to focus on others, circumstances or ourselves. How often will we struggle and whisper, *"All* Joy, Lord?"

But when these times come, we can back up, regain our perspective, accept His appointed way forward and contemplate His coming:

For momentary, light affliction is producing for us an eternal weight of glory far beyond all comparison, while we look not at the things which are seen, but at the things which are not seen; for the things which are seen are temporal, but the things which are not seen are eternal (2 Corinthians 4:17,18).

Therefore, since we have so great a cloud of witnesses surrounding us, let us also lay aside every encumbrance, and the sin which so easily entangles us, and let us run with endurance the race that is set before us, fixing our eyes on Jesus, the author and perfecter of faith, who for the joy set before Him endured the cross, despising the shame, and has sat down at the right hand of the throne of God (Hebrews 12:1, 2).

We will need healthy doses of patience, prayer and correcting until He comes! There is a great deal of fine tuning to be done. But if we will focus on the Lord and live by the light He has given, our joy will indeed be full.